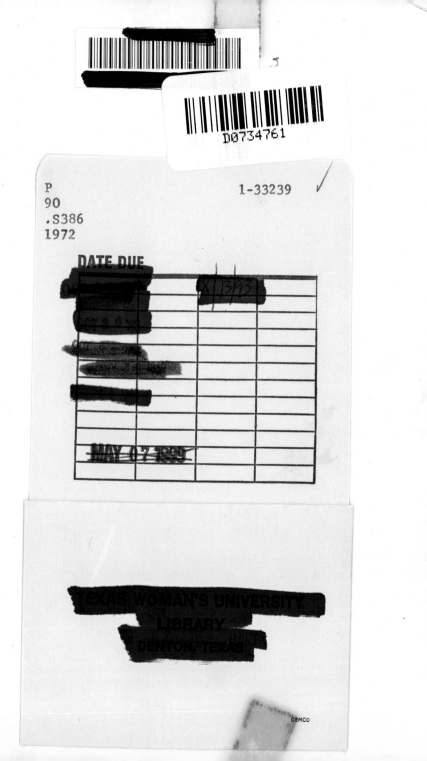

# COMMUNICATIONS
# IN
# CRISIS

# COMMUNICATIONS IN CRISIS

by

## Paul A. Schreivogel

Thomas Nelson Inc.

Nashville • New York • Camden

All rights reserved under International and Pan-American
Conventions. Published in Nashville,Tennessee, by
Thomas Nelson Inc. and simultaneously in Don Mills, Ontario,
by Thomas Nelson & Sons (Canada) Limited.

*Library of Congress Catalog Card Number: 79-147913*
*ISBN: 0-8407-5031-5*

Printed in the United States of America

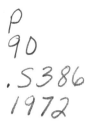

## DEDICATION

*"To the most uncommon
of women, Nancy: wife,
mother, woman—often
at the same time"*

# COMMUNICATIONS
# IN
# CRISIS

# 1

(a sort of introduction to this print experience)

# MAKING
# A CONNECTION

## MAKING A CONNECTION

> There isn't any particular relationship between all the messages, except that the author has chosen them carefully, so that, when seen all at once, they produce an image of life that is beautiful and surprising and deep. There is no beginning, no middle, no end, no suspense, no moral, no causes, no effects. What we love in our books are the depths of many marvelous moments seen all at one time.
>
> Kurt Vonnegut, Jr., *Slaughterhouse-Five*

Communicating involves reaching out to touch another element of life and digging into one's interior to understand one's self. It is the task of "making a connection," struggling to connect with a friend, a god, or the personal self. Being involved in communication means being connected with life, "the depths of many marvelous moments," every minute one is alive.

## WALLED-IN MAN

Man has a habit of building a wall around himself, a protective barrier damming up his ego and selfhood from the assaults of the world, even when he may be growing and developing inside. The paradox of man building personal walls to protect himself while attempting to grow to new understandings creates crazy-quilt patterns of communication confusion.

In each age man has followed these paradoxical roads, protection and expansion, and in each age there have been crises in communication. These crises may have been deeply personal, involving friend, wife, lover, neighbor, or quite distant, particularly in cultural and environmental change, political and institutional upheaval, and national priorities.

Self-constructed personal battlements are sometimes necessary for people, but all too often these walls prevent the openness and contact which can enable one to be more humanistic and which can free one to live and communicate with a sensitivity for the dignity of others.

## MAN IN THE PRESENT AGE

Man has always been the architect of his age. Any particular age may be reflected in the intensity of the crises in which it is involved. The present crisis in communications is represented by speed, acceleration, the instant exposure to any joy or sorrow anywhere in the world, in which millions of people can share a mass trauma at one moment in space and time that can seriously affect the most personal of relationships. New powers are available for people to sense and realize the type of world they live in. While the past was often deceptive, the present and future have potential for revelation. We will be able to take soundings of the health of the world, from the beat of our neighborhood to the constant drum roll of far-off places.

Today 80 percent of all the world's scientists who ever

walked the earth from the beginning of time are alive and working; soon young people will be wrapped in formal education from age three to age thirty-five; a war in Asia and Africa becomes a continuing soap opera on the six o'clock news; a dance invented in a far corner of the world one evening is danced by young people at the local high school the next evening.

It is that kind of world man has created; one in which new tunes are being played by people caught in urban complexes.

The Age of Aquarius is not yet present. People must still battle to make connections, communicate with one another, and fight to have communications media and culture serve rather than shape people.


## ABOUT THIS EXPERIENCE

It is difficult to add anything new to all the thoughts about communications in today's world. Philosophies, concepts, and ideas about communicating have been shared and studied in living rooms, on television, and in classrooms. There is very little that we might do, except, perhaps, to view the problem from a new perspective, or derive an innovative thought from someone's unique presentation of it.

It is important to understand the problems of communication in a new light, for today all humans are involved in history making. It is being recorded before their eyes; they are participants in events which will shape the future of the world.

It is too easy in this morass system of modern complexities to have fear and ignorance overtake sensibility. It is too easy for the individual to build his walls higher and higher, obstructing all chance of communicating with others.

This book, with its juxtapositioned print concepts and images, testifies that the world is indeed complex, but with understanding and patience one may untangle the threads and experience both the problems and the avenues for newer understandings.

The understanding of one's culture, the environments present in that culture, the language in motion, and the process of communicating will offer clues to the crisis present in our world. Answers are not given; these must be found by each individual within his own experience.

This book attempts to operate as the human does, thinking simultaneously in a variety of avenues, offering evidence of the worlds we live in.

It is a world in which early man lived his tribal culture in face-to-face living relationship with his neighbor. Meaning and life ended at the boundary of the village. He learned realities from his neighbor—the voice, the bodily expression, the very style of living.

Later, man lived with Gutenberg and his printing press, taking the very personal world of the tribe and placing the experience into a world of private consciousness. The world become dominated by the book, printed words frozen onto paper with no sounds, no immediacy. The book recalled past history, robbed emotion, provided few new experiences. Tears, love, home, friendships, and so forth, became private; rooms and buildings were constructed for the privacy of the book, rooms in which a sneeze became a form of heresy.

13

In the present age, full of the fast beat of the proton, man is shaken from his privacy to live simultaneously with his neighbor. The probing eye and ear of radio and television force one to live with many realities at the same time, an at-onceness in which everything is constantly taking on new forms, but never achieving a final shape, an illogical world in which crisp definitions of the past soften as they take on new meanings. The suburbanite's picture window with its grassy images is disturbed by the television screen with its images of war and poverty; the slum dweller sees what he has been robbed of through the eyes of his old black and white television set.

The actual is upon us. One can look, see, and feel what is happening. A child of twelve in 1970 has already experienced this book. He has lived through seventy-two hours of the tragedy of JFK, twenty-four hours of MLK, eighteen hours of RFK, besides the visual experiences of Viet Nam, the moon, political conventions, and Saturday morning toy sales. He knows of change, illogical worlds, multi-languages, and death.

The world of the young today is the world of the present; the world of the old is the world of the past. The intense desire for both to make connections with each other can take place as each realizes his role in his culture and environment. Communication involves sensitivity, an openness for people to accept people, even as nations must learn eventually to accept nations.

## AND SO . . .

. . . this book is offered to a world in which old truths are taking on new meanings; where the flickering images of *Woodstock* delight and threaten; and where the dot patterns

14

of television invade the retina of the family room; here images are more important than realities; newspapers are the textbooks for new myths; and people are trying to make sense of themselves and their world while trips to the moon hover in the background.

Communications in crisis is the reality. But even realities change. It is hoped that a reader, via this experience, may be led to new realities, convinced that communication is possible and all crises are not bad, and, finally, that he may develop a new ability for making connections in the midst of new realities.

# PART ONE

# NOTES ON CULTURE

**1.**

Humans have a peculiar characteristic. They tend to live as though life in their society is the same as that of other societies. They assume that ethics, morals, and tastes of their society are universal.

**2.**

The common way of life in a society is called its *culture;* it includes the rituals, customs, and beliefs of the society.

**3.**

Many anthropologists have said culture is that complex whole which includes knowledge, belief, art, law, morals, custom, and any other capabilities and habits acquired by man as a member of society.

## 4.

The root of the word "culture" means to equip, train, foster, or cultivate, thus "agriculture" means the training of the soil. The most fertile soil for any culture is its children; it is through them that society's codes are channeled, generation after generation.

## 5.

Culture becomes the tradition of the society. It invades and supports the behavior of society, particularly the various social, religious, artistic, and ideological patterns. Culture seeks a permanency through its prevailing institutions.

Three weeks ago I asked my children, "What did you do in school today?" Their answer was, "Nothing." Then I realized the truth of their response. John and Carol did nothing in school, school did everything to them.

"We begin with children. It is imperative to catch them in time. Without the most thorough and rapid brainwashing their dirty minds would see through our dirty tricks. Children are not yet fools, but we shall turn them into imbeciles like ourselves, with high I.Q.s if possible.
    R. D. Laing, *The Politics of Experience*

## 6.

There are different cultures throughout the world. America has its own unique cultural style, as do Spain, Egypt, India, and other countries. Western civilization has many common cultural traits. For instance, the Judaic-Christian tradition may be found in both European and American cultures.

## 7.

It is difficult to recognize our culture when we are living in the midst of it. This is especially true if we have been "cultivated" since birth in that culture.

When I was a child my culture taught me that
black people came to this country in 1619 in
slave ships, a Civil War was fought over blacks,
and a few blacks made it, like George Washington
Carver. Then I grew up and found out what my
culture left out.

*I suppose the Christian cultural concept of
going to heaven when you are good and to
hell when you are bad is the reason our culture punishes wrongdoers rather than re-
forming them.*

**8.**

The best way to know our own culture is to take a look at ourselves from the outside, from the eyes of those who don't have a vested interest in our culture. Thus the French can validly comment on our war policies, the Swedes on our slums, and the Africans on our frightening money power.

**9.**

Within culture there are smaller cultures, or subcultures. Subcultures develop because groups within the dominant culture have common interests and life-styles. Thus one easily finds a youth subculture seeking out an independent role in the midst of the dominant culture.

**10.**

In recent years subcultures have become recognized as valid expressions of groups seeking their identity within the strong dominant culture. In the United States the culture of white Anglo-Saxon Protestants is being prodded by the black, the Mexican-American, the male-dominated female—all vibrant subcultures.

When applying for a new position I was asked to describe myself. I told the interviewer to speak to my wife, she knows me better than I do.

## 11.

The threat of subcultures within the society will often lead to subtle repressions. Subcultures are often seen as minority groups, lacking in number and power, thus easily oppressed by the majority culture.

## 12.

Animals have no culture, man does. Culture regards the world not as an object, but as an idea and purpose. Animals are instinctive, the world to them is merely an object.

## 13.

Culture changes by encountering a new age and new people. Those caught in this change often experience conflict and tension: innovative ideas, creative viewpoints, and pioneering individuals threaten old cultures; institutions begin to feel the prickly irritation of new worlds.

**"Black is Beautiful"**
**"Male Chauvinist Pig"**
**"Huelga"**
**"Make Love, Not War"**

Whenever the politician or minister berates me about sticking with the past I feel that tradition takes on the character of an ingrown toenail.

27

**14.**

Cultural change is experienced as the farmer's plow confronts the industrial assembly line. It is the mechanical age rubbing against the electric cord, providing sparks which join old and new patterns.

**15.**

Culture is a movement. It is inherited from the past, lived out in the present, and it charges into the future. Those who do not know this, who would want culture stable and unchanging, find cultural change traumatic.

**16.**

"Cultural shock" occurs when present realities and future hopes are ignored for the sake of the past. Fear, ignorance, and prejudice are often among the causes for this. Making children be Xerox copies of the past retards the potential of culture to change and grow.

*I often feel like an American innocent in my own culture. I desire to raise my children with integrity, guiding them toward making choices, developing within their souls a humanistic spirit. My culture, though, says my children are good if they achieve the proper grades, go to church, fly the flag, and not make waves, even if their cultural ark is sinking.*

In 1939 I listened to the <u>Lone Ranger</u> on radio, in 1968 I saw the <u>Lone Ranger</u> on television, by 2000 I may be the <u>Lone Ranger</u>.

## 17.

A culture is composed of people of all ages, each contributing to the cultural totality. When one age group is silenced the entire culture suffers. A sense of history suffers when the old are carted off to retirement villages, idealism fades when youth are repressed, stability vanishes when the middle-aged are ignored.

## 18.

"Cultural deprivation" happens when different segments of the culture lose contact with one another: the poor having no relationship with the middle class; the young never facing the old; minorities avoiding or being avoided by the majority.

John boldly faced me and said, "Dad, when I'm in college you and I are going to be in different generations." John is nine years old.

The small girl presses her nose
against the car window and
screams, "Look mommy, see the man
with the black head."

## 19.

Culture is complex, offering those who seek to do so the opportunity to choose their life patterns. Culture is flexible; today's stigma may be tomorrow's virtue.

## 20.

Culture demands action—the support of the good, the changing of the outdated.

## 21.

Culture demands risk—the willingness to be open to innovation as a creative element of life.

## 22.

American culture "assumes" from its heritage that there is political freedom, universal education, the satisfaction of material needs. It must now assure these advantages as it assures full humanity for all its people. The same must be done in all cultures.

An educator recently told me a book she banned from the library ten years ago is now on the reading list of all the literature classes.

## 23.

The search for full humanity implies a need for cooperation rather than competition, for trust rather than fear, for responsive government instead of lobby-laden cocktail parties, for life instead of death-dealing war, for living, not just surviving.

## 24.

Changes in culture, no matter how slow, imply the recognition and understanding of new languages rising out of the needs of new people.

The boy was ten, his dad nearly forty. Together they viewed man's first step on the moon. Dad recalled his Flash Gordon and Buck Rogers days. The boy has lived as if rockets existed since creation. Dad said, "Fantastic, beautiful," as the man stepped on the surface of the moon. The boy asked, "What took him so long to get there?"

**25.**

The seeds of change are always found in past cultural patterns. The old culture encourages change, either through openness which allows change or repression which forces change.

**26.**

Cultural change is encouraged by the variety of languages needed to communicate within a culture. A crisis in communication occurs at the point of "interface," the overlapping of cultures and generations.

**27.**

Cultural language itself creates tension and change. There is the language of the electron and the book; the language of female and male, rich and poor; the language of phonetic expression and visual perception; the language of clothing for creative expression.

## 28.

Language is the mode of travel in culture, connecting people with the needs of the culture and transmitting the content of culture to others. Language is the medium binding the culture to past and present and encouraging culture to be involved in change.

## 29.

Within our culture there are many languages, some new, others old, all in need of communication and interpretation. Word and body are primary languages which change as we extend ourselves beyond our territory via telephone and telegraph.

*Language often confuses. Why is the Upper Nile River south and the Lower Nile River north? Do people in Clear Lake, Iowa, go uptown or downtown when they shop? Why are adventurous and demanding experiences condemned while things that are considered in good taste are always boring?*

## 30.

Clothing is a language, having evolved from mere protective utility to expressive form of personality. Language in today's society takes the form of visual experiences and juxtapositioned images.

## 31.

The complexity of cultural change, language diffusion, and environmental bombardments have combined to accelerate a crisis in communication, a clashing of innocent peoples caught up in cultural upheaval, and that's what this book is about.

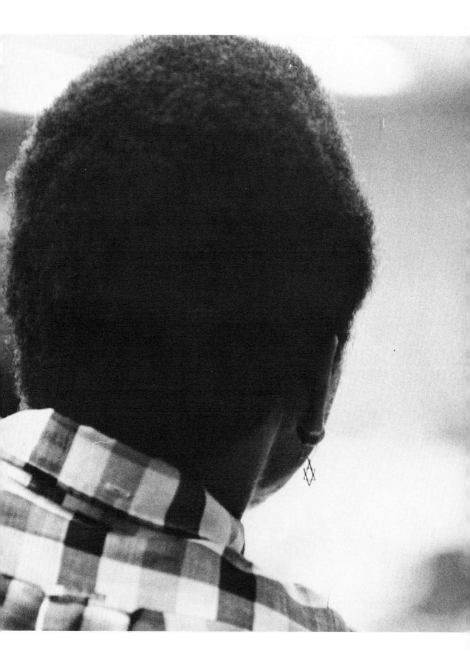

**III**

# NOTES ON ENVIRONMENT

## 32.

Environments are those surrounding conditions and influences which affect the existence and development of people, society, and ultimately, culture. In understanding environment one would begin to understand the total aggregate which influences humanity and creates the changes which take place in culture, including the mores, laws, religions, language, and life patterns of people.

## 33.

Most people think of environment in terms of nature: wind and rain, ice and snow, sun and sand. "Natural determinism" once was believed to control the destiny of man. It was thought that nature affected man's culture.

My son was concerned about an environment. He asked me, "What is heaven like, and where is it?" I said, "Look around you, son, look around you."

## 34.

Natural environments have only a fringe effect upon cultures. The Eskimo is able to overcome his natural hardships and the Pacific Islander is able to live fairly comfortably in his environment, except for the occasional hurricane. Man is able to control and predict weather, reverse the flow of rivers, develop synthetic clothing, and construct housing which overcomes natural drawbacks.

## 35.

Man's control over nature is evidence of his ability to destroy what he controls, to exploit and kill potential for good. And so the air is polluted with auto fumes, beaches baptized with crude oil, rivers laced with mercury compounds.

## 36.

Hidden amid the concern for redeeming the natural environment are new environments which are radically determining the future of man, changing his language, governments, and long-held beliefs.

## 37.

Technology has created the invisible environment of the "electric life." Humanity is riding an electric surf, a trip carrying people to new worlds, pinching nerves in spinal cables, surrounding humanity with the envelope of the proton.

"Through the electronic media of television, telegraph, or telephone, man has equipped his modern world with a nervous system simulating the one in his own body."

(Stewart V. Lancaster)

## 38.

The electronic environment of man is a massive bubble. It is perhaps best seen in Telstar circling the earth, wrapping it in a giant package of positives and negatives, forcing man to speak to and learn from others, and to create a global community.

## 39.

The technological environment is the new environment. It prompts an "electric determinism" for all people. It introduces new sensations to old cultures, forces an interface between the good old days and the new days. It is sometimes noisy, often quiet, but usually so soft that it massages us into change.

## 40.

Technology offers man "environmental media," media which have become extensions of man's spinal cord, man's inventiveness, which have created the acceleration of man's need to change his culture.

## 41.

Understanding environmental media helps man to understand himself, sense changes in language and communication. But environmental media may also lead man to apathy, culture shock, the inability to face issues, and an insensitivity to life itself.

My son views the evening news, Walter Cronkite sharing the world with a nine-year-old child. In the midst of the commercials there is a three minute interlude offering the saga of Viet Nam. My son turns to me and asks, "Dad, do I have to go to Viet Nam when I grow up?"

## 42.

Environmental media have placed people and their cultures in motion, creating activity fields which make nothing the same anymore. No thing is as it was. This morning's war becomes this evening's entertainment.

## 43.

The electronic age has placed people in motion, culture in change, the world into complexity.

President Kennedy's assassination was rerun so often it looked like a segment from <u>Mannix</u>.

The world today is no longer measured in terms of B.C. or A.D., but rather by BTV and ATV. Children constantly ask, "What was the world like before television?" Today contact lenses are taken for granted, eyesight is no longer measured by the standard of 20/20 vision, but rather by the size of the tube, 18-inch or 20-inch.

## 44.

Old images are being seen in new ways, traditional religions are being questioned, political intrigues are being rejected by new, perceptive peoples. Electronic environment is speeding the transition from old worlds to new worlds. The new Columbus is the electrical circuit.

## 45.

The electronic environment is creating new cultural artifacts which convey new meanings through film, television, telephone, Telstar, radio. They change the mood of traditional media such as newspapers, books, and magazines.

57

## 46.

The new environment of electricity is changing the meaning of clothes and hair; the modes of transportation; the uses and value of money. It binds together subcultures for new combined powers to change society: women, blacks, Indians, and youth form new organic unities in culture.

## 47.

Environmental media shapes culture. It bands differing world cultures together into new spiritual unities, and tears apart old territories for new concerns.

The world has certainly changed. The credit card has replaced the two-dollar bill as the new gamble; letters were personal and are now pica; fluid words are frozen in time; film has become an art; television has replaced the old "B" movie as mass entertainment.

## 48.

The aggregate of these new electronic environments enfolds and surrounds us like a hidden coral reef wraps itself around an island, ever present, always expanding, often unnoticed.

## 49.

Human worlds are flooded by the stimuli of electronic nerves offering new communication codes. New Jericho trumpets, electrically charged, make sounds which change and rebuild the walls of old cultures.

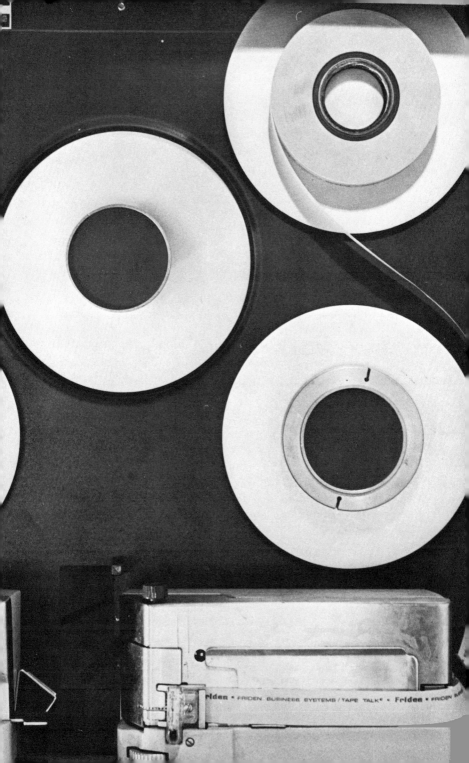

## 50.

The new environments are containers for people who have been tuned up by chemical nuances, speeded along by electrical circuits, buffeted by hope and fear, becoming confused so that nothing is like it was yesterday, not even the image of a god.

## 51.

All-at-once people read the newspaper while viewing *Gunsmoke* with the sound of the radio in the distance, answering the telephone while above their heads an airplane is being hi-jacked to cigar-shaped islands . . . and all the time the spiritual voice of Lenny Bruce echoes with laughter, because he told us about the scene and we didn't believe him.

*I often wondered what happens in local communities during the commercial break of a Super Bowl football game. Sewers and electrical circuits become overloaded, water pressure lowers. All because people take those few moments to go to the bathroom or to make some popcorn. Each activity forces communities to reexamine and change utility systems. The electronic cathode tube forces governmental cooperation and new expenses, all because 22 men grunt and groan on a particular Sunday.*

## 52.

The Americans, Russians, and Chinese are bound together in this electronic environment by sticky satellite tape crisscrossing the heavens. It's an electronic bunting of peeping toms saying everything to everybody simultaneously. And those cultures, nations, and people who refuse to heed the environment, who stand outside the container, are lost in fear and ignorance.

## 53.

Electronic environments remove young and old from earthly vacuums to cosmic realities and complexities, from the personal to the interpersonal, monologue to dialogue, from old normalities, and that is not bad.

It is a curious phenomena of our society that with every school, church, and fire station we build, we also construct a mental health clinic. Meanwhile we're saturated with group therapy and sensitivity training.

## 54.

If culture is the sum total of the common values of people, then the new electric environments are the catalysts for changing the culture, for electric media are causing people to take a look at their values and their institutions.

## 55.

Nothing seems as it was because leisure, politics, religion, philosophy, everything changes as the world changes. The key to understanding these changes is to know the environment, to subvert false pride and face new worlds, and to hope in a future. Each baby born in these new environments offers a reprieve for mankind . . . each new life makes the immediate transition from the Stone Age to the Twentieth Century, into an electric roller coaster of life and death.

My daughter grasps my hand and says, "Daddy,
I love, I love, I love." She is the hope for the new
cultures that I must grow to understand in my old
age. I hope at that time I may look ahead and say,
"I love, I love, I love," even to those movements
which will be unknown to my generation.

# IV

# NOTES ON LANGUAGE

## 56.

Language is a system used by societies to express and communicate thoughts and feelings, allowing people to interact. It is a commonality of sounds and images associated with ideas and emotions.

## 57.

Language is as old as human society and is used to express whatever a culture requires of it. It may be complicated or simple, depending upon the needs of the culture. Language increases or decreases according to culture. A culture which is complex and highly sophisticated offers much more variety in its language.

*I have often felt that writing about language is like being a mosquito in a nudist colony: it is difficult to know where to begin.*

"A new language is seldom welcomed by the old."
(Edmund Carpenter)

## 58.

Language may open or it may limit a man's horizons in the world. A person may know only those parts of existence to which he limits his language. One who limits his language to a particular subculture confines his vision and hope.

## 59.

Human speech is a primary language, one in which man attempts to locate himself and his place in the world through phonetic expression, forming sounds related to feelings and objects. Through cultural training of language, one learns that the phonetic combinations which produce the word "c-a-r" stand for a particular type of vehicle.

The National Association for Bureaucrats recently presented its humorous "Order of the Bird" award to a professor for using this language form: "given a syntactically ambiguous grammar, it is possible to use semantic information to disambiluate its syntax and construct a similar unambiguous grammar."

## 60.

Print is a secondary form of language. It is an attempt to freeze on paper (or stone) the thoughts of man, a plastic form without the expression of spoken language, devoid of the power of verbal or physical communication. Nevertheless stationary symbols of print represent avenues of understanding and bear the content of culture and ideas.

Spiroisms:
"nattering nabobs of negativism"
"pusillanimous pussyfooting"
"hopeless hysterical hypochrondriacs"
"troglodytic leftists"
"effete snobs"
"organ-grinders of the old elite"
"pablum for the permissivists"

## 61.

Sign language are signals which replace spoken or written words, as seen in conversations between deaf mutes or the tourist attempting to get a bargain in a foreign country.

## 62.

All cultures offer other language possibilities for communication. The history and life of ancient cultures may be perceived via the language of pottery, sculpture, etchings, and primitive paintings on cave walls.

## 63.

In contemporary society the art media still retain their value as language. The artist attempts to speak of the world he sees and feels with his own particular skill. Through the span of Pablo Picasso's works, societies may experience, in the language of brush and pen, the changes and problems of mankind.

## 64.

Film and television contain their own history, style, and visual grammar. They also create a language for culture, the new language of the technological society. These two communication media are still in the process of being understood and interpreted.

## 65.

Cultures and people do not exist in vacuums. When culture changes or a particular language becomes inadequate to express meaning sufficiently, new languages form, or old ones are resurrected.

The communications of artists is still relatively unnoticed in society. Public panderers such as sports heroes and glib TV personalities are more observed and admired than the artist and his message. Perhaps this is good; it may allow the artist to be the quiet conscience of society.

In our rush to live out life rapidly, patience has given in to speed in the new forms of language we create. If we understood that our threescore and ten years is but a moment of eternity, we might take the time to relax, slow down, and know our languages.

## 66.

Hair has once again become a language, the outward expression of inner feelings. Throughout history man was usually free to wear long hair and beards for the sake of fashion, convenience, or self-expression. In recent wars, men were encased in womblike trenches and unsightly helmets, so hair had to be cut short. The "clean-cut" type also became a symbol of the masculine male, the warlike hero. The youth subculture has created a turnabout which is now being emulated by the older generation. After much foolish harassment, long hair and beards are becoming acceptable in many quarters of society. The old human language of hair is being revived within the old culture and is creating subtle changes in the culture.

"If it has a beard it is a man; if it doesn't
have a beard it is a woman."
    (Old Spanish Proverb)

## 67.

The recording of history has created a new historical language, oral history. The decline of letter writing and handwritten memos and the rise of electronic communications has forced history to be compiled from tapes, interviews, and films rather than from painted sources as in the past.

## 68.

Language can make slaves of people, particularly those who become ensnarled by sayings, clichés, and the imprisonment of proper "grammar." Man's language ought to flow out of his cultural and personal possibilities.

## 69.

All languages are mass media, used by masses of people most of the time; the English language is the most common of mass media.

*"What do you want, good grammar or good taste?"*

## 70.

Fashion is a mass media language reflecting the personalities of people. Clothing helps to define sex; it reflects a world of personal experiences or a social group; it produces fear in some, shock in others, but is a kind of celebration for most.

## 71.

The secondary language of print has traditionally produced books, newspapers, magazines, handbills, billboards, and a host of other materials from which thoughts are Xeroxed on the mind. The recent revival of free presses with the "underground newspapers" have enabled young people to discover new meanings in printed words.

It is possible that mass media has reached a saturation point. Perhaps technology reached its heights with the Model T Ford and has gone downhill ever since. Is it possible that mankind's movement toward mass innovation reached its peak with the utterance of its first word—which may have been "help."

# 72.

Animals also have a language; they communicate with adults as well as with other animals. Animal language is different, though, because it expresses only subjective feelings, not rational thoughts. There is an instinctive naturalness about animal language.

# 73.

In the animal world a dog always talks like a dog, even if raised by cats; a bird will always chirp as birds do, even if they are raised in a home of humans. In the human world a Chinese person raised in America will speak pure "Americanese," and an American born and raised in Egypt may speak fluent Arabic. A child raised in a strange culture will naturally adapt that culture's mode of communication as if the language were his own.

"Remind me to write an article
on the compulsive reading of
the news. The Theme will be
that most neuroses can be
traced to the unhealthy habit
of wallowing in the troubles of
five billion strangers."

Robert A. Heinlein
<u>Stranger in a Strange Land</u>

One must wonder why American soldiers in Indochina refer to inhabitants of that beautiful area as "gooks?" It appears the American often assumes the "American way of life," with its culture and language, is superior or "elitist." Such name-calling shows an insensitivity to other cultures and languages.

# As we all know, the mentally retarded can only make baskets and other simple objects like...

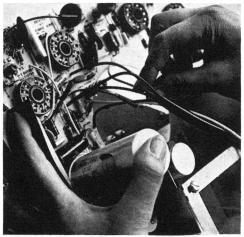

Computer subassemblies.
Printed circuits for electronic
test sets.
Electric meters.
Automobile instrument panels.
Aircraft components.
Hospital supplies.
You already know that the
retarded worker is generally
more conscientious, loyal and
punctual than the average
employee.
Perhaps you have a few
"simple" jobs he might do in
your business.

For information about
employing the retarded, write
The President's Committee
on Mental Retardation,
Washington, D.C. 20201.

## 74.

Language is complex today because educational systems avoid the realities of languages prevalent in the world. Speech is natural to the human, but schools first teach children to read and write. Children are raised with television, yet most schools almost deny the existence of television unless it affords a didactic propagandist motif to brainwash, a visual aid for conformity.

"What did you do tonight, son?"
"I took a trip around the world."
"What?"
"Yeh, I watched television."

## 75.

There is no set rule for language except the perceptive awareness of the many languages which daily enclose each person. Languages are constant contributors to the life and realities of the growing earth. Growth ceases only when the individual builds walls.

# NOTES ON COMMUNICATION V

## 76.

Communication is an action process taking place in time and space. It is influenced by culture and personal experience and shaped by events that are happening simultaneously. Communication is taken for granted many times; often one notices it only when it fails.

## 77.

Communication demands sensitivity to the times; to the personal meaning each human carries within himself; to the varieties of avenues by which communication takes place. And it requires an awareness of the many languages surrounding each person.

## 78.

All people interpret communication according to their experience. Caution is necessary in interpreting another's remarks. Thought should be given as to how one would be interpreted.

i
know
you believe
you understand
what you think
i said
but i'm not sure
you realize
that
what you heard
is not
what i meant

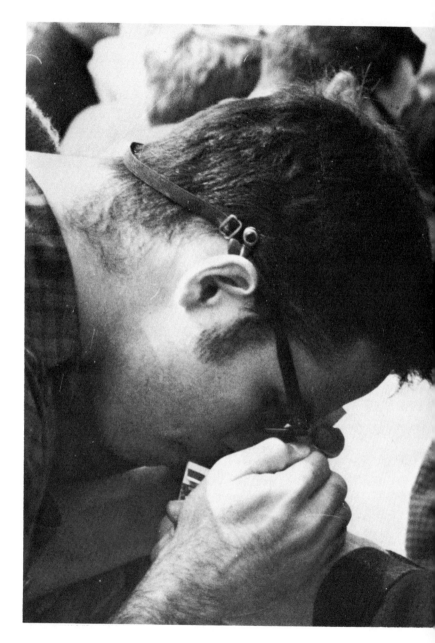

## 79.

Verbal communication, face-to-face, is the easiest and most personal form. Words may be changed, corrected, forgiven, forgotten.

## 80.

Nonverbal communication may radically affect verbal connections. Facial expressions or gesture may support or deny the meaning of the spoken word; it is difficult to change a flush of anger or a glaring eye with soothing or phony words.

"What happens during the unspoken
dialogue between two people can never
be put right by anything they say—
not even if, with mutual insight into
what has occurred, they should make
a joint attempt at reparation."
    (Dag Hammarskjöld)

Many people forget that one must "mean" what he
says. Message and gesture must agree or the meaning
of the message is lost.

# 81.

Verbal and nonverbal communication is affected by the "noise" of life. "Noise" would be those things which influence our communication: personal experiences; political viewpoint; social status; financial power; theological or philosophical stance; emotional stability; prejudices; anything that makes us what we are.

# 82.

"Noise" in communication also affects *interposed* relationships, those situations in which a barrier is placed between those who communicate.

## 83.

In a telephone call the phone and the distance is placed between two people, affecting the type of conversation which occurs. The clerical collar of a clergyman or the desk of the businessman represent an institutional barrier, or at least an awareness, when two people converse.

It is interesting to note how many business meetings now take place on the golf course or in the cocktail lounge, or the number of clergymen forsaking the formal collar in order to remove the institutional image from the presence of two people attempting to make a connection.

# 84.

Face-to-face communication, verbal and non-verbal, begins in the interior of each person. All people absorb the world within themselves, subjecting it to their intellect and emotions. This interior world is a hall of culture and environment, personal like and dislikes.

# 85.

Communication becomes the externalizing of inner feelings, sharing emotion and information with someone else, a way of getting our inside outside ourselves.

# 86.

The selection of the words and supportive systems of nonverbal actions ultimately become the language of communication.

# 87.

The meaning of the communication comes from the person speaking, and words are only a part of the message. Words have only definitions, people have meaning. People then must keep talking, until the verbal and nonverbal clues come through. Then communication begins to take place.

# 88.

Feedback, the response to one's communication, informs a person whether or not the communication has been received. A sender of a message must also be a good listener to pick out the clues as to whether his message came across.

Too many ministers' sermons are like God's mercy—everlasting. Churchgoers should be able to respond immediately to a sermon, to ask the meanings of words, or simply to ask what the minister means. One failure of the sermon is that preachers speak of distant problems and causes that hardly relate to the reality of the local community. They don't want to "step on toes" or lose any contributions.

# 89.

The social context of communication will determine the content of the message. Communication varies when one talks to a wife, a neighbor, a political friend, or an opponent. Words change meaning in each situation. The word "democracy" has different meanings for a member of the S.D.S., the John Birch Society, a Communist, a Republican, or a young person.

How many can you identify:

SDS, LBJ, MPAA, ADC, SST, LSD, ABM, OEO, ADA, RPM, M*A*S*H, TVA, CBS, NFC, NHL, AC, VW, STP, J, HHH, IBM, DOA, IV. This is the new language of contemporary society—who needs words?

## 90.

Mass media is communication. It offers message to people, informing, propagandizing, entertaining, and generally speaking at people. There is very little feedback and exchange with mass media. In the communication process mass media is hampered because of the lack of feedback and exchange between sender and receiver.

## 91.

Mass media seldom offers new ideas or concepts. It generally reinforces traditions of the past. New technology and new media generally are used in familiar ways until the media is understood.

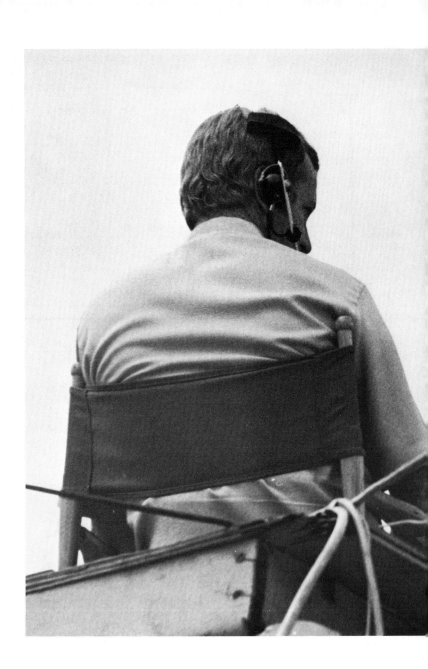

## 92.

Television drama, entertainment, and information programs follow old patterns and formats. Most comedy, situation dramas, quiz shows, and soap operas, are patterned after radio techniques. So-called specials often imitate old vaudeville styles.

## 93.

Mass media is an outlet for opinion makers, people who attempt to influence the masses and later hope to confront people face-to-face, particularly in the arena of politics. Politicians and radicals use media for the same purposes, as a means to get the masses to think they represent the thoughts of important segments of people in the land.

"The idiots who used to squat, mindless, blind, impassive, before the squawk box of their radio, indifferently imbibing pap and poison, canned laughter and soap opera, got their great boon a decade or so ago from Almighty God and General Sarnoff. Damnation was total, eternal. The television era had begun."

Samuel Elam

## 94.

Communication breakdown happens when people refuse to: listen and observe and be sensitive to the realities which surround everyone; refuse to feed back their understanding to arrive at clearer meanings; assume a message has been given or received; use cliché-laden language and worn-out phrases to impress rather than to communicate and mean something; refuse to seek the truth in any given situation; neglect to understand there is no objectivity anywhere in the world, that every message and report is the subjective response to some experience.

## 95.

How man communicates will determine his meaning and his survival. Unless relationships between man, at the most primary levels, become humanistic, the world's problems will never be solved. No war will be prevented until neighbor is able to communicate with neighbor in the same apartment building.

"We should have a great many fewer disputes in the world if words were taken for what they are, the signs of our ideas only, and not for things themselves."

John Locke

VI

PART TWO

THE LANGUAGE
OF WORDS

## BLUM

Dog means dog
And cat means cat;
And there are lots
Of words like that.

A cart's a cart
To pull or shove,
A plate's a plate
To eat off of.

But there are other
Words I say
When I am left
Alone to play.

Blum is one.
Blum is a word
That very few
Have ever heard.

I like to say it,
"Blum, Blum, Blum—"
I do it loud
Or in a hum.

All by itself
It's nice to sing:
It does not mean
A single thing.

It would be impossible for human beings to live in any form of harmony if they could not talk to one another. In spite of the mass confusion of languages, even within a common language beset with dialects and differing word meanings, talking is essential toward community stability. Sharing ideas and feelings is the crux of sensitive community living. The ideas of Jesus and Socrates were shared by verbal communication, these two great men having never placed their own thoughts in writing.

From the beginning of time, man has been talking, creating a mouthy atmosphere which shall remain to the end of time. The mouth becomes a funnel to knit together the fabric of mankind, committing man to marriage, love, business dealings, hate, friendships, and, unfortunately, the institution of war.

The world of words may be found in every society, the more complicated the society the more words it will formulate to express its experience. Such expansion of words may be seen in the fact that the King James Bible used 7,000 different words to communicate its vivid literature and sensitive poetry. English Bard William Shakespeare used 24,000 words in combinations to provide history with a vast resource of literary art.

Today a college graduate has a minimum working knowledge of 40,000 words with a supportive base of another 40,000 words. If one searches a dictionary for information he will find more than 260,000 entries. Though the average person may use only 3,000 words in daily conversation, 500 of these words frequently have more than 14,000 definitions. And these definitions constantly fluctuate. A few years ago the words "Hot Pants" meant a condition, today they mean a fashion.

In addition to the number of words available to the human community, mankind also confuses the issue of communication with approximately 3,000 different languages, not counting the various dialects available within these languages. Though most people in the United States speak English as a common language there are still goodly numbers who communicate in German, Italian, Chinese, French, Yiddish, Portugese, and Spanish, which uniquely happens to be the native language of the State of California.

Added to the complexity of human discourse is the rhetoric which emerges from social and political movements, the advertising world, sub-cultures, and the special disciplines of sociology, religion, and science. Each make their contribution toward the curse of Babel, the diffusion and confusion of words in the human condition.

Words, like people, do not live in a vacuum, but are bombarded by varieties of experience, ricocheting from meaning to meaning, being adapted to new environments, participating in the process of change as much as humans, suffering its own forms of future shock.

Perhaps the merry-go-round of words experienced by people is best demonstrated in the entries of Samuel Elam's book, *Hornbook For The Double Damned.* In this book Elam lists a basic vocabulary for the "solid citizen." His first entry is: "Analysis: see Psycho." Upon looking further in the dictionary, one finds the following listing: "Psycho: see Analysis."

The crisis of words in contemporary society is the crisis of meaning and content. Most people forget words do not have meaning in themselves; the meanings are to be found in the people who use the words. Words never carry the total message, but are extensions of the messages contained within people.

A minister or church who preaches *love* as a word from a pulpit but allows gossip, hate, slander, or racism to exist in the church has conflict between the word "love" and the content of the church's life. The medium, the minister or church, is the message. If the medium's message is different from the "word message", the word message loses its meaning, it has no content.

A further example may be found in many aspects of the educational system which teaches young people the principles of democracy, praising its attributes, yet having the educational system operate an authoritarian system. The "word message" of the educator is lost in the content of the system, one which disavows democracy from being practiced in the system.

People become important when attempting to decipher words. The feelings, emotions, lifestyles, history, and environment of a person ought to be known in order to understand the message of the person.

By trying to find out what people mean when they use words the communication process gives way to human interaction in which people confront one another as humans rather than as chattering computers spewing forth unreceived or unperceived messages. When people or institutions use words as verbal cliches, labels, and dogmas, apart from meanings and people, then separation occurs between people and institutions.

*America, Love It or Leave It* and *Make Love Not War* are such dogmatic verbal cliches which alienate two groups of people. These slogans represent a literate attitude toward serious problems and tend to excuse the need for the talking and listening and understanding which must be experienced for human intercourse. In this case words separate rather than join, antagonize rather than unite, destroy meaning rather than supply content, dehumanize rather than humanize.

All words offer a point of view, a stance from which one perceives the world which surrounds him. An understanding of that world view and that person may be experienced through selection of words. The meanings take shape as words form and the satellite activity of body expression takes place.

Difficulties in communications may be traced to word games people play. The following words used by differing peoples offer double meanings, depending upon one's location in the environment:

> PEACE: this is what our side is for and the other side is against, unless, of course, you belong to the other side.

> ATROCITY: this is a miscalculation, an error, that is, if you are an American and your boys commit the atrocity (oops, I mean error).

> PATIENCE: a white man's word which means another 300-year wait for the black man, unless it involves a suburban tax cut.

> COMPROMISE: a politician's word which simply means, "I make a compromise, he makes a shady deal."

> JUNK: an antique, which is someone else's junk, unless

you are selling it, then it becomes confusing.

Sub-cultures contribute a selection of words to mainstream language forcing dictionaries to expand every few years. These words have become fixations among certain strata of American culture:

*rapping:* conversation, not necessarily communication.
*shrink:* a psychiatrist.
*bells:* neither church nor liberty, but pants.
*bread:* Adam Smith called this money.
*straights:* strictly suburban, or the opposite of bells.

Many old words gain new meanings as society experiences new traumas. The following old words have taken on new meanings and concepts:

PIG  BLACK  CHAUVINISM  HONKY  FLICKS  VIBES
BAG  PILL  TURN ON  LIB  RIGHT ON  BEAUTIFUL
WAR CRIME (In Calley's case)

Other old words are merely resurrected from a forgotten past, their old meanings becoming again usuable:

*Environment  Ecology  Charisma  Credibility Gap
Super Star* (anything from TV to Jesus Christ)


Religion as a typical institution of mankind has had its problems with words, particularly the differing Christian churches and their relationship to the verb "to be", a verb which creates a drastic separation among people claiming the ultimate theme of love.

Holy Communion, the symbolic meal of love of the Christian church, is the great dividing meal because of the verb

131

"is". The churches suffer a literate problem, divorcing meaning and content of an event for the precise meaning of a word, a fact which appears incongruous to their faiths. A literate cannibalistic argument has replaced a concern for unity in a love feast of people seeking the same apparent goals in life. Whether the food taken at the meal "is" real body or blood (sic.) or represents the same (sic.) seems a far cry from the original intent of the meal, an event which has roots deep in the heart of the Jewish Passover as a meal of remembrance.

An obscene word is usually a word which is offensive to someone's modesty, and may be a word which generally upsets most of the people of a society much of the time. Though rejected when used publicly, an obscene word may be acceptable once the majority of society uses the word in a common vulgar form. One only need remember the horror expressed when Clark Gable (as Rhett Butler) concluded the film *Gone With The Wind* with the words, "Frankly, my dear, I don't give a *damn*." Today, the word "damn" is used openly and freely at every level of society, having replaced its old substitutes: "danged", "darned", and "doomed".

There were few obscenities in early societies. Generally, these ancient civilizations had "holy words" which people were careful not to use because of sacred associations. These words would often be depicted by symbols. The early Jews and Arabs used signs for "god" rather then speak or write the word. The advent of Christianity encouraged the use of verbal censorship, the banning of certain words which did not belong in the "holy" realm.

Tracing the roots of an obscene word is difficult, even determining why certain words are considered obscene is obscure. Words such as "damn" and "hell" were formerly banned because of theological association. Today, as these words lose their theological relationship and the Victorian prohibitions of the past slowly fade, these words have become generally acceptable in conversation, film, television, and books.

The question of obscenity will continue to irritate society and raise questions whether any word can be considered obscene in the context of a particular situation. *Fanny Hill,* a classic of pornography, contains no obscene or "dirty" words, yet is vivid pornography. D. H. Lawrence uses obscenities in *Lady Chatterly's Lover* and this book is considered by many critics and students of literature a great piece of literary work.

It has been suggested, in the ivy covered halls of colleges that some words be eliminated from one's vocabulary in order to shrink the complexity of words now found in one's speech patterns. It is interesting to note that as one finds the English speaking "properly" and the French speaking "precisely", the American may be found speaking "profusely", constantly seeking fertile ground to invent and implement new words into language.

One suggestion relates to eliminating such rhetoric as "white-anglo-saxon-protestant", "captains of culture", "status-seeking" and all those words which end with "orient", such as "people-oriented", and "western-oriented". Such words might be as irrelevant as calling someone "commie" everytime a new concept is offered in opposition to the standard form. Even the words "ghetto" and "slum" need revision as they are used so interchangeably by journalist and politician, one is no longer sure of the content of the words, either historically or in the contemporary vein.

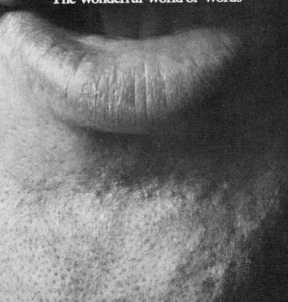

The Wonderful World of Words

Human beings come in all sizes, a variety of colors, in different ages, and with unique, complex and changing personalities.

So do words.

There are tall, skinny words and short, fat ones, and strong ones and weak ones, and boy words and girl words and so on.

For instance, title, lattice, latitude, lily, tattle, Illinois and intellect are all lean and lanky. While these words get their height partly out of "t's" and "l's" and "i's", other words are tall and skinny without a lot of ascenders and descenders. Take, for example, Abraham, peninsula and ellipsis, all tall.

Here are some nice short-fat words: hog, yogurt, bomb, pot, bonbon, acne, plump, sop and slobber.

Sometimes a word gets its size from what it means but sometimes it's just how the word sounds. Acne is a short-fat word even though pimple, with which it is associated, is a puny word.

Puny words are not the same as feminine words. Feminine words are such as tissue, slipper, cute, squeamish, peek, flutter, gauze and cumulus. Masculine words are like bourbon, rupture, oak, cartel, steak and socks. Words can mean the same thing and be of the opposite sex. Naked is masculine, but nude is feminine.

Sex isn't always a clear-cut yes-or-no thing on upper Madison Avenue or Division Street, and there are words like that, too. On a fencing team, for instance, a man may compete with a sabre and that is definitely a masculine word. Because it is also a sword of sorts, an épée is also a boy word, but you know how it is with épées.

Just as feminine words are not necessarily puny words, masculine words are not necessarily muscular. Muscular words are thrust, earth, girder, ingot, cask, Leo, ale, bulldozer, sledge and thug. Fullback is very muscular; quarterback is masculine but not especially muscular.

Words have colors, too.

Red: fire, passion, explode, smash,

murder, rape, lightning, attack.

Green: moss, brook, cool, comfort, meander, solitude, hammock.

Black: glower, agitate, funeral, dictator, anarchy, thunder, tomb, somber, cloak.

Beige: unctuous, abstruse, surrender, clerk, conform, observe, float.

San Francisco is a red city, Cleveland is beige, Asheville is green and Buffalo is black.

Shout is red, persuade is green, rave is black and listen is beige.

Oklahoma is brown, Florida is yellow, Virginia is light blue and Massachusetts is dark green, almost black. Although they were all Red, at one point Khrushchev was red-red, Castro orange, Mao Tse-tung gray and Kadar black as hate.

**One of the more useful characteristics of words is their age.**

There's youth in go, pancake, hamburger, bat, ball, frog, air, surprise, morning and tickle. Middle age brings abrupt, moderate, agree, shade, stroll and uncertain. Fragile, lavender, astringent, acerbic, fern, velvet, lace, worn and Packard are old. There never was a young Packard, not even the touring car.

Mostly, religion is old. Prayer, vespers, choir, Joshua, Judges, Ruth and cathedral are all old. Once, temple was older than cathedral and it still is in some parts of the world, but in the United States, temple is now fairly young. Rocker is younger than it used to be, too.

Saturday, the seventh day of the week, is young while Sunday, the first day of the week, is old. Night is old, and so, although more old people die in the hours of the morning just before the dawn, we call that part of the morning, incorrectly, night.

Some words are worried and some radiate disgusting self-confidence. Pill, ulcer, twitch, itch, stomach and seek are all worried words. Confident, smug words are like proud, lavish, major, divine, state, dare, ignore, demand. Suburb used to be a smug word and still is in some parts of the country, but not so much

around New York anymore. Brooklyn, by the way, is a confident word and everyone knows the Bronx is a worried word. Joe is confident; Horace is worried.

**Now about shapes.**

For round products, round companies or round ideas use dot, bob, melon, loquacious, hock, bubble and bald. Square words are, for instance, box, cramp, sunk, block and even ankle. Ohio is round but Iowa, a similar word, is square but not as square as Nebraska. Boston is, too—not as square as Nebraska, but about like Iowa. The roundest city is, of course, Oslo.

Some words are clearly oblong. Obscure is oblong (it is also beige) and so are platter and meditation (which is also middle-aged). Lavish, which as we saw is self-confident, is also oblong. The most oblong lake is Ontario, even more than Michigan, which is also surprisingly muscular for an oblong, though not nearly as strong as Huron, which is more stocky. Lake Pontchartrain is almost a straight line. Lake Como is round and very short and fat. Lake Erie is worried.

Some words are shaped like Rorschach ink blots. Like drool, plot, mediocre, involvement, liquid, amoeba and phlegm.

At first blush (which is young), fast words seem to come from a common stem (which is puny). For example, dash, flash, bash and brash are all fast words. However, ash, hash and gnash are all slow. Flush is changing. It used to be slow, somewhat like sluice, but it is getting faster. Both are wet words, as is Flushing, which is really quite dry compared to New Canaan, which sounds drier but is much wetter. Wilkinsburg, as you would expect, is dry, square, old and light gray. But back to motion.

Raid, rocket, piccolo, hound, bee and rob are fast words. Guard, drizzle, lard, cow, sloth, muck and damp are slow words. Fast words are often young and slow words old, but not always. Hamburger is young but slow, especially when uncooked.

Astringent is old but fast. Black is old, and yellow—nearly opposite on the spectrum—is young, but orange and brown are nearly next to each other and orange is just as young as yellow while brown is only middle-aged. Further, purple, though darker than lavender, is not as old; however, it is much slower than violet, which is extremely fast.

Because it's darker, purple is often softer than lavender, even though it is younger. Lavender is actually a rather hard word. Not as hard as rock, edge, point, corner, jaw, trooper, frigid or trumpet, but hard nevertheless. Lamb, lip, thud, sofa, fuzz, stuff, froth and madam are soft. Although they are the same thing, timpani are harder than kettle drums, partly because drum is a soft word (it is also fat and slow) and as pots and pans go, kettle is one of the softer.

**There is a point to all of this.**

Ours is a business of imagination. We are employed to make corporations personable, to make useful products desirable, to clarify ideas, to create friendships in the mass for our employers.

We have great power to do these things. We have power through art and photography and graphics and typography and all the visual elements that are part of the finished advertisement or the published publicity release.

And these are great powers. Often it is true that one picture is worth ten thousand words.

But not necessarily worth one word.

The *right* word.

## MARSTELLER INC.

Burson-Marsteller
Marsteller International
Medical Group • The Zlowe Company

Advertising • Public Relations
Marketing Research

Chicago • Los Angeles • New York
Pittsburgh • Washington, D.C.

Brussels • Geneva • London
Paris • Stockholm • Stuttgart • Toronto

The recent explosion of the visual experience in communications will never replace words. Contrary to the thoughts of some, the old Chinese proverb, "A picture is worth a thousand words", was a ploy to excuse the facts of illiteracy rather than highlight the communication value of pictures. The visual experience may help enhance the power of words, forcing society to be more selective in its use of words and display increasing concern related to the content of a message.

What must be avoided in verbal communication is the experience of such men as Everett Dirksen, late United States Senator from Illinois. Senator Dirksen was the master of jargon and verbal usage. He knew people were more interested in seeing a Senator than listening to his words. Mr. Dirksen, in a masterful manner, seldom constructed a logical sentence or used good grammar; he simply made a good impression upon the audience. His black horn-rimmed glasses, flowering hair, impressive but often meaningless words, somehow convinced the audience they had really heard something, when all they did receive was an image.

People may again capture the significance of words as information if words free themselves from the frozen heritage of print and enter the stream of human consciousness as personal and community expressions of communication. More may be experienced in the conversational flow of words between two people than in the stilted reading habits of a private room.

It is important for people to keep talking and keep listening, attempting to reverse the flow of the Tower of Babel mentality. Such communication may happen as people . . .

talk, talk, talk

Talk can arouse,
but of itself
it cannot heal.

To listen—
*truly* listen—
is to begin
the healing process
a wounded nation needs.

Listen to the wind.
Listen to the birds.
Listen to the trees.
Be still,

and listen to your God.

Above all, listen to
your own conscience.
This is the beginning
of listening.

Then—
listen to one person.
Even for five minutes.
Each day.

If each of us in the
United States *listened*
with all his might
for just 5 minutes

each day, wouldn't
we be a healthier nation
for it?

What this country needs
is a good 5-minute
listener.

You?

I'm a listener

a. leave grammatical rules to the ivory towers of scholarship and high school classrooms. There are no such things as good words or bad words, or the correct form of expressing self, as long as understanding and communication take place. Communication has no rules. If a double negative assists the task of communication, use it, forget the English teacher!

b. listen to words being spoken and not anticipate the direction and content of someone's speech, thus leaving open avenues for misinterpretation of what is being said. Clear away prejudice that you may listen freely to the words and meanings being sent your way.

c. know the fabric of the world in which they live as well as the environments experienced by the people they communicate with. Communication occurs in a complex world, part of knowing what is being said is attempting to decipher the basic question of communication . . . "what do you mean?"

d. avoid assumptions, namely that people hear you when you speak or understand the message. Constantly ask if your meanings are being received, if people know you, so they know your words.

e. fill in their lives with information. Read newspapers, be involved with books, listen in on other conversations. These are avenues for expanding your own horizons, developing personal growth, increasing knowledge and experience. As one's mind and experiences expand so do the possibilities for expanding powers of communication.

f. speak with candor, openly and honestly. There is nothing wrong with expressing personal opinion or sharing personal value judgments, as long as one recognizes they are subjective views. Don't worry about giving offense. Constant avoidance of truth and disagreement dulls the creative thinking powers of an individual.

# VII

# THE LANGUAGE OF TELEVISION

Each environment of man offers a capsule image of the total world. One's world view becomes the sum total of the various capsule images one experiences in his lifetime. The medium of television has offered man a confusing array of capsule images, images which have overburdened him with varying patterns of information and entertainment. This mosaic of tiny abstractions offers a wide view of mankind which is sometimes true, other times distorted.

Television is a gift of the electronic age, it provides new environments for the living room. It is the "people's media", having high ratings, serving as chief source of news information, and retaining overall dominance of the other media. There are presently 677 television stations in the United States, and this figure increases each year, particularly with the advent of Cable Television. It has been estimated that children view 15,000 hours of television in the first twenty-one years of life, and that the average person's life includes a total time of nine years of television viewing. The magazine with the largest circulation is devoted exclusively to television (*TV Guide,* 14 million weekly). It took 80 years for the telephone to be installed in 34 million homes, yet television made that great stride in less than ten years.

The images created by television enlighten and disturb the population. The decade of the 60's offered vivid proof of the power and trauma of television upon the psyche of people. That decade transformed the world from a stage in which people were actors to a television documentary where people became real participants in a global village.

The 60's, an era of turbulence and transformation, was widely exposed to the retina of mankind; the foibles, faults, and celebrations of man were present for all to share. Realities and disturbing ideas were more traumatic than the soap opera or the contrived morality of *Bonanza.*

The working man of 1959 who retired in 1970 and the young child born in 1959 and who entered the sixth grade in 1970 shared a visual journey of disillusionment and joy as the events of the 60's jumped into their nervous systems. In the 60's people were kept aware of what lies beyond the normal experience of life through the television tube. Television demonstrated the facts of multiple revolutions existing at the same time; showed life as basically illogical; challenged all to make sense of the wide world of life with some base of personal integrity and concern.

In the 60's television fused the electric proton with the spinal cord, a linkage which broke the silence of man in the world, paradoxically asking man at once to walk on the moon and to purchase cheese products.

The path of the 60's . . .
*Harvest of Shame* opens the decade; 34 die in the Watts riot; an undeclared war spills blood onto the living room carpet; four young men from England create mass hysteria; a new frontier is discovered on the moon; two brothers and a black leader brutally murdered; a funeral of a Pope (1970 already experienced an attack upon a Pope); a Vietnam police chief cooly blows out the brains of a Viet Cong; an Eisenhower marries, so does a Johnson and a Sinatra; open-heart surgery; black fists raised high in protest on an Olympic podium; the flower and bayonet meet in Chicago; Johnny Carson, Dick Van Dyke, Green Acres, Gunsmoke, Tom Jones, Sid Caesar; *Hunger U.S.A.* closes out the decade.

Only time will reveal whether the 70's and 80's will expose communities to the similar traumas of the 60's. Only time will reveal whether the people's media will visually oversaturate toward apathy or spur on the community toward change. One frightening fact is revealed of the 60's. The decade opened with *Harvest of Shame* and closed with *Hunger U.S.A.* It was apparent not much happened to assist the people who formed the content of these two programs.

The word "television" is composed of two parts: *tele* means "far" and *vision* means "to see". Television is "seeing from a distance," a far shot of the world carried to near sighted people.

The distant view massages our local bodies, moves our emotions and intellect and stimulates new thoughts. It makes old information new to those who didn't know the information existed. And while revealing the need for change, it also gives evidence that most public institutions prevent change from happening. We found, for example, that not all policemen are good and that political conventions are essentially un-democratic and boring; thus television alters the old images achieved from radio and newspaper. The fact that a distant person can be viewed as an important local personality taught the radical revolutionary what the politician had already learned: In order to receive wide coverage and make yourself appear more important than you are you must make the early evening news broadcast.

Television also has the power to destroy time and space, as well as memory. Distant places, geographical and histori-cal, flow into the mind with contemporary ease. The medium offers instant *retrieval* of information. One no longer needs to remember man walked on the moon, for television, like the computer, *stores* the information and *relays* it to the viewer, always *in the present.* The event no longer need remain in the mind, stored in a section of the brain for future use, television serves as the memory bank for mankind.

"We have temporarily lost
our slide informing you
we have temporarily lost
our picture."

Television bombards the atmosphere with an *electric* language which offers size and depth and can be measured and weighed. It is the language of electric technology. Television signals are transmitted through space by radio carrier waves, similar to radio, except that television light signals are converted into electric signals, transmitted to a distant place, then converted back to a light signal.

The Federal Communications Commission assigns radio "bands" in order to avoid communications confusion. These bands are similar to highway systems. Radio uses narrow bands (sound only) and television uses wide bands (sight and sound), which might be likened to the use of two-lane and six-lane highways. The bands on which signals are carried are called "frequency bands" or *channels.* UHF (ultra high frequency) has seventy channels while VHF (very high frequency) has twelve channels, a total of 82 channels available for television broadcasting.

The television image is an optical illusion. The ability of the eye to retain an image while looking at another image creates the illusion of movement, this is called "persistence of vision."

The cathode-ray tube in the television set glows brightly when hit by electrons. A charge pattern is set up on the screen composed of minute dots arranged horizontally across the screen. The dots have varying patterns which ultimately create the images on the face of the tube.

An electronic beam, a scanner, scans the dot patterns at a uniform speed from left to right. The beam rapidly scans alternate lines (262½ each time), covering 525 horizontal lines thirty times a second, or a total of 15,750 lines per second, creating sixty frames (pictures) per second.

The amount of lines scanned per second form the frames, which in turn the eyes "read" and creates the illusion of movement. Thus television operates much like film, where the frames pass before the eyes at a rate of 24 frames per second in order to create the illusion of "moving pictures."

The television image is constantly being formed, sculpturing new images for the eyes to encounter; it offers, as Marshall McLuhan states, "a mosaic mesh of light and dark spots" in which the viewer is kinetically involved in forming the image, forcing more involvement with television than any other media.

The process itself becomes an electric communication between man and machine because of the constant overlapping of the electron and the eye simultaneously forming the visual. Electric language quietly enmeshes the electric cable and the spinal cord.

Such involvement with this medium can weave man and machine into one, to the point of determining what kind of values, culture, and language man will have. Mankind is faced, then, with an electric determinism. Perhaps Don Fabun was correct when he mentioned in his delightful magazine, "It was, more than anything else, TV that did in this country." (*The Children of Change,* Kaiser Aluminum News)

Television is not a new medium of the past twenty years. Milton Berle appeared on a snowy screen in an experimental television program in 1929. The Berlin Olympics, 1936, were the first sports events to be televised, the events being beamed to 3,000 people in specially constructed halls. President Roosevelt was seen on television in 1939 opening the New York World's Fair.

Television's explosion came in the post World War II period, particularly the 50s when mass production allowed for mass consumption. By the 60s it has been estimated the average person in the United States was viewing at least 2½ hours of television a day.

The important communications event of the 60s was the launching of Telstar, allowing for world wide video communication. Now it was possible to carry into the living room a live war from a distant place.

Television's entry into the latter part of this century will provide radical changes in the electric process as well as in the social and political areas. The tube may become more personal, increasingly informational, and decidedly dangerous. The danger is to institutions as people gain more knowledge and also for people as institutions gain more power.

Cable Television (CATV) will alter the course of television the next ten years, offering variety in visual content as well as the possibility of two-way communication with the station. CATV is the entrance of television signals into the home via a cable rather than air waves. The cable may be linked to the telephone line in each home, with a monthly subscription charge for programming and maintenance. For people who do not subscribe to such service the local community meeting hall or a church could be wired for cable.

CATV will offer many more channels, with the opportunity for local communities to initiate their own programming, offering "narrow casting", reaching special community groups, as opposed to "broadcasting" which is designed for mass participation. CATV will relegate the television antenna to the role of an artifact of another age.

CATV has the possibility of being a forum for community self-expression and may generate community dialogue, perhaps returning the communities of America to the Town Hall concept of its earlier days. Besides this, the world of CATV will include the possibility of taking music lessons in the home; conducting bank transactions from the living room; tune in to congressional hearings; provide psychiatric care with direct vocal communication with the doctor; offer sewing lessons, neighborhood news; send and receive personal letters; order groceries from the local supermarket; request special programs for individual viewing in the home; provide outlet for local drama groups.

CATV has its negative aspects. Closed-circuit channels may already be found in banks and department stores standing a vigilant watch over people. A Philadelphia museum is able to observe every corner of its building through one control board. It is possible to place cameras on lamposts and observe the citizenry in action. Such observations may lead to "people tapping", similar to telephone wiretapping which has been on the increase in recent years.

Perhaps the next amendment for the United States Constitution may be for an "Electronic Bill of Rights" to protect the individual from outside visual intrusion into private life

148

and activity. Such a "bill" would aid in hampering the increasing involvement by government and industry into the private lives of people by large data collection banks.

The advent of cassettes now allows the public to visit the local department store and purchase or rent a particular television program. A converter unit will be automatically built into the television set to allow instant play of visual images on the television screen. The cassette fosters development of individual tastes for leisure and provides a creative outlet for new forms of communication. Cassettes will be purchased and stored as are books and records. A number of book and record companies are considering a "cassette-of-the-month" purchase plan. Cassettes will then begin to affect the law. What has been formerly censored from the public airwaves, such as pornography, may now be viewed in the privacy of the home, making many laws unenforceable. Such availability of diverse forms of home programming will allow the television set the freedom now shared by magazines and books, being able to purchase the experience one desires without national or local censorship.

The team of CATV and cassettes will assist in changing society. It will be possible for all minority groups to receive and share information in new ways, changing people and ideas. Political parties, racial groups, writers, housewives, children, business companies, and artists will have new sources of information. Nothing will be the same anymore; the world, even the day-to-day living experiences, expanding of the human consciousness, and even the dangers of overt propaganda through these new forms of electric exposure, will change people, force new tensions, and hopefully, encourage humanity to reach for the continued quest for freedom.

The electric signals which stimulate the senses are converted to electronic probes, a language of information loading the mind with the heaven of advertisements, the hell of the news, canned laughter, dramatic kaleidoscopes, indepth analysis, and a myriad of images which corrupt and erupt man into a new consciousness.

Singer-composer Mason Williams has said of television, "Television doesn't have a job, it just goofs off all day." Even Vice-President Spiro Agnew has had a field day using television as a personal dart board. With all the criticism of television from varying sources, people still watch and enjoy much of what they see. The question facing any medium is whether it can be artful and creative and at the same time serve the mass audience. Mass audiences tend to lower the creative level of culture, having to face the problem of reaching the low brow and the high brow in the same time period.

The electronic probes which enter people's homes at the present time are geared toward the middlebrow, or, more succinctly, the middle class. Most drama, words, and values found on television are of middle class mentality; and this group is not generally noted for its receptivity to change or creative culture.

The middle-class approach forces television to add canned laughter to primitive country humor or explanatory notes to offerings of fine culture. For this reason television takes on middle-class characteristics. The technocrat middle-class supports *Mission Impossible;* the program, *Bonanza* serves to support middle-class value systems.

Television then begins to reinforce value systems of the past upon the people of the present. The black man, sitting in his slum apartment seeks the values and materials he sees whites using, yet these values are really old, thus he is torn in a new conflict. He desires what he sees, when he receives it he discovers that what the whites had was not that important to the meaning of man. The dramatic content of television programming tends to shape and form through constant repitition. The family life of *Bonanza,* the sharp dileneation between good and evil, the solution approach toward problems . . . each works on the viewer, creating a Mary Poppins approach to life, a fantasy land of old environments butting against the realities of the present.

Some of the values of television create phantom lands for the viewer, an artificial paradise into which the viewer imagines himself, wishing that life were that way, but it isn't. The "rear view mirror" approach sneaks its way into program content, seeing the present in terms of past culture. Yet the present and future are different worlds, worlds which make one mad, sad, and glad, all simultaneously . . . the old world only makes us wishful, the nostalgia of wishful thinking, recalling the world that really never was.

Often it is the news which creates trauma for American society. The news reflects the events of the day, and these events touch more than the middle-class. The news, in its attempt to inform and remain free, smacks headlong into middle-class politics, values, and lifestyles, disturbing those who want to remain undisturbed. When the news carried conflict from distant places into homes, there was very little antagonism created in the country; but when the news began to demonstrate that the same events happened in our own backyard people balked and began to attack television.

The news created a mirror of life which few dramatic shows offer, and many people disliked what they saw. The 6 o'clock news revealed that students wanted democracy in

151

# Should TV cover it, or cover it up?

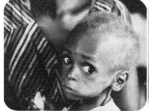

COVER IT ☐ DON'T ☐

COVER IT ☐ DON'T ☐

COVER IT ☐ DON'T ☐

COVER IT ☐ DON'T ☐

COVER IT ☐ DON'T ☐

COVER IT ☐ DON'T ☐

COVER IT ☐ DON'T ☐

COVER IT ☐ DON'T ☐

COVER IT ☐ DON'T ☐

"If television would only stop showing all that bad news, maybe we wouldn't have so much of it." Sound familiar?

Think of the questions it raises:

If television is to black out riots, should it also black out UN debates? School demonstrations? Battle scenes? Political speeches? Who will be the censor to tell us what news television should cover, and what news it should cover up? And would covering up a bad situation remove it? Or make it worse?

The answers are found in our tradition of a free press— guaranteed by the First Amendment to the Constitution. It recognizes that the people have the right to know everything that matters to them—the bad as well as the good. Only a public that knows the facts can make wise decisions.

Television, by being free to cover all the news, has increased our awareness of the problems of our schools, our cities, our world. And television, like the rest of the press, must remain free. For if, out of fear of public disfavor or government reprisal, newsmen, broadcasters or newspapers fail to report what is happening, the freedom of all of us is diminished.

As Walter Lippmann wrote, "The theory of a free press is that the truth will emerge from free reporting and free discussion."

For broadcasters, "covering it up" might mean playing it safe. But television would not be doing its job. Because you have the right to know.

## Television Information Office
## of the National Association of Broadcasters
745 FIFTH AVENUE, NEW YORK, N.Y. 10022

education; that minorities sought equality in jobs; that violence was really an American tradition. In this way news became an important segment of electronic language, an irritating ethnic language probing the realities of life, removing the veneer of innocence. In a sense, the news demonstrated that people were not innocent and that God had to lose his mask for people to gain reality.

A typical thirty minute news broadcast cannot provide in-depth coverage, but must rely on presenting the basic facts of an event. Time limitations and the constancy of advertising enable a broadcaster to use about as many words as may be found on two thirds of the front page of a newspaper.

Within these limitations the news, the lifeblood of democracy, must be delivered to the viewers, for it is the right of viewers in an open society to have access of information.

Walter Cronkite, CBS newscaster, pointed to the importance and freedom of news in a speech before the National Association of Broadcasters in Chicago, 1970:

> "It is human nature to avoid confronting the unpleasant. No one wants to hear 'our boys' are capable of war crimes, that elected officials are capable of deceit or worse. I think I can safely say that there are few of us who want to report such things. But as professional journalists we have no more discretion in whether to report or not to report when confronted with the fact than does a doctor in deciding to remove a gangrenous limb.

> "If it happened, the people are to know. There is no condition that can be imposed on that dictum without placing between the people and the truth a barrier of censorship at once as fallible and corrupt as only self-serving

men can make it.

"The barrier can be built by government overtly by dictatorship or covertly with propaganda on the political stump, with harassment by subpoena, with abuse of licensing power."

Weakness in news broadcasting occurs when the news media avoids their responsibility: by overplaying the small incident and failure to report the whole event; by encouraging a personality cult for the newscaster which tends to focus the report of the news on the content of the reporter; by failing to distinguish editorial comment or interpretation from the general news.

The news is a window to the world and a reflection of each person, revealing strengths and frailties. As it reports, and sometimes, because of the nature of the medium, entertains, it conceives images in conflict with personal images and creates the tensions necessary for an informed, free, and hopeful people. Freedom of the news is a fact never achieved, but rather a reality which must be constantly sought by the public and by the news media itself.

Television has become the chief means for hawking goods. Advertising agencies literally assist in subsidizing television, alerting people to new products, including politicians, and creating needs for people most of whom have had their real needs satisfied.

A news announcer reports a story of life and death and then a soap commercial flashes on the screen, making soap as important as life and death. The television commercial appeals to basic instincts in man which offers false images of what a human being is or could be as they employ images of sexuality, class distinction, snobbery, and obsolesence.

The language of television advertising encourages viewers to bounce from product to product. Buy more time-saving products and take more time to earn money to save time, an endless circle of dialectical materialism.

Advertising is closely related to political campaigning in the process of selling a candidate. Today the political candidate is packaged for the public as much as an underarm deodorant. The planners of the Nixon campaign in 1968 had this to say, "We have to be very clear on this point: that the response is to the image, not the man." The packaging of a candidate is much easier than visually attacking another candidate. The 1970 political campaigns experienced several incidents where specific candidates were attacked via slanderous labels or dubious relationships. In most cases this type of advertising failed, creating antagonism on the part of the electorate toward the candidate doing the attacking. The electorate may be easily sold on a particular candidate, but appears to have some perceptions when personal attacks are created against a candidate.

Truth in lending laws may be needed to protect the common citizen from political packaging. If men and women must gain political position via image creating rather than personal content, then the society is in deep political difficulty.

Though the common television viewer may often complain about the content of the medium, their motivational comments differ radically from their behavioral actions. What people say and what they do are at opposite poles. No matter how sharply people tell poll tabulators they prefer "culture" on television, the people still view and enjoy current offerings.

Presently television serves as babysitter, entertainer, and information producer. If people want television to change they must then seriously begin to mesh lives with the electric and informational language of the medium, then allow their voices to be heard in the hallowed halls of televisionland. Such voices may be heard if concern is expressed in some of these ways . . .

a. For many years television served as a come on, an enticer, seeking viewers to lull and buy. Viewers may change such relationship by expressing their views to television people, local and national. The letter is read and the phone call received at television studios. Such contacts ought to praise as well as criticize, encourage as well as discourage. This also implies sharing your views with the Federal Communications Commission.

b. Be selective in viewing programs. Plan programs in advance through the weekly television guide in the local newspaper. Strive for balance in viewing, including viewing and supporting the local National Educational Television programs.

c. Involve oneself in local hearings for Cable Television franchise in local communities. Insure fairness of programming for local community concerns, education, and community services. Request the CATV to have a local board of community representatives who are composed of a real cross section of the community, including minority groups in order to affirm the desire for community programming.

d. Develop program suggestions for local CATV, including such items as presentation by local drama groups, consumer information, live school board meetings, religious celebrations, youth programs, city council meetings, athletic events, etc.

e. Read the local television critic for insights into programs, also follow the words of television critics on the national scene. In time it will be possible to recognize critics who share the same taste and thus serve as a general guide toward understanding of program content.

f. When you dislike something . . . turn it off.

# VIII

# THE LANGUAGE OF FILM

The language of film is a reel world of fantasy and escape, a medium for education and propaganda, and the most explosive art form of the 20th century. Film is a medium which has captured the fancy of millions of people. This medium is a new stylized world in which young and old can be film makers and artists, taking 8mm and 16mm cameras in hand to record the world as they see it.

Movie theaters today offer endless varieties of film. Film study is flowering in high school curriculums alongside literature and painting. Film programs have replaced college lecture series. Adult evening education programs offer film study alongside flower arranging classes. Community film festivals are growing, not only New York and Chicago, but also Dallas, Atlanta and Rochester are participating. Film criticism and film scripts have given rise to new literature on bookshelf racks at the local drugstore (*Easy Rider, Salesman*). Many artists contend that the finest literature and music today is being written for the screen, the film script being the new form of the novel.

Film has involved itself in interesting events in local history, two of which involved a President. Newspapers reported that Richard Nixon, after viewing *Patton:* several times, made his dramatic decision to enter Cambodia, also, prior to making a public statement about the guilt of a defendant in a trial which was in progress, President Nixon had viewed the film *Chisum,* a tough John Wayne western with strong law and order motif.

Sports also came into the film arena. Woody Hayes, Ohio State University football coach, usually has his team view a film the night before a game. In 1969, prior to the Ohio State-Minnesota game, his team viewed *Easy Rider.* Coach Hayes said the next day, "We weren't ready to hit." The 1970 film choice before the big Ohio State-Michigan game pleased him; it was a western film, *Monte Walsh.*

Film audiences in recent years have also changed. *Time* magazine reports that 62% of today's moviegoers are between the ages of 12 and 30, are better educated, more selective, and drastically smaller in number than the mass audience that supported old Hollywood films.

French film maker Jean-Luc Godard has called film "truth twenty-four times a second". There is no question today that this is perhaps true in some way for every film viewer. Film may educate and entertain and prick the conscience out of apathy. It can transmit images to collide with the images of the mind, forming new values and new thoughts.

Films are parables, offering 90-minute stories to engage our 70-year lives. They may be real in the truths they communicate, but are fantasy in the manner in which the truths are portrayed.

The world of film offers its initial impact because it is a "total environment." A choice is made to go to a theater; the darkened theater pushes out other distractions. There are no other competing environments such as may be found when viewing television where one may be surrounded by books, newspapers, children, paintings, and general family room clutter. In the movie house even the popcorn becomes part of the total environment. Movies are immersions into the flickering pool of screen images. The theater wraps the viewer into an engrossing cocoon, one which has made film the art form of this century, a medium to be contended with in the changing culture.

Young and old are being rubbed with breaths of new

vision as well as new avenues for debate with such items as: *Alice's Restaurant,* which offers a hymn of joy and sorrow to the hippie culture, doing a better job than journalistic exploiters of informing the public of this segment of society; *Medium Cool,* revealing the problems of news media, particularly the photographer, in recording public events; *Z* and *The Confession,* demonstrating the power of left and right political followers to ultimately squash free expression; *Catch 22* showing the insanity of people at war; *The Sand Pebbles,* a film of past and present truths related to colonialism; *Mary Poppins,* combining fun and fantasy for an audience who realizes fantasy is important to the human condition; *Airport,* proof that tense drama may be good entertainment, even when it is a "B" movie; *2001: A Space Odyssey,* showing that, as one critic stated, "If it can be thought or written it can be filmed; *Rachel Rachel,* the experience of a lonely person seeking some relationship in her personal world; *Joe,* sharing a myth of "hard hats" as brutal unthinking people.

Film is less than 100 years old, having its birth in the first commercial showing in a small cafe in Paris, France, in 1895. Very little has changed in film language since its first few decades as a visual art, the major changes being technological. These changes include sophisticated styles of splitting screens, larger images, multi screens, new lenses. Being a technological art it makes sense that the new experiences visually in this medium emanate from the field of technology.

For those who feel current films create community concern, they only need to recall D. W. Griffith's film *The Birth of a Nation,* released in 1915. This film, a fine experience except for the stereotyped role given Negroes, created racial tension in major cities of the country, spurred congressional debate, and cost $2.00 a seat to see.

The language of film is grammatical, just as much as is the language of literature. The visual language, developed by early film makers, include such elements as the cut, dissolve, panning, the long shot, the close-up shot, and the creative technique of animation. To know the visual impact of the power of film is also to realize the skills of the language which tell the story. The language offers the intellectual and emotional impact of a scene or sequence.

The language of film was developed through its brief but powerful history. Film was pioneered by such men as D. W. Griffith, the great American film director, who introduced the basic elements of visual language as well as making films with significant content. Russian film maker Sergei Eisenstein demonstrated the power of film as propaganda in such mass epic films as *Potemkin.* The unique contribution of the documentary film was introduced by Robert Flaherty with such productions as *Nanook of the North* and *Man of Aran.*

The underground or experimental film offered artists subterranean film experiences, films which were not produced for mass entertainment. Instead they attempted new film concepts and dealt with ideas the general public was not ready to accept. Underground films were being made since the time film was born. In contemporary underground films one finds such subjects as drugs and the erotic, as well as experiments with computer made images.

As early film makers trained the eye to see they also taught the mind values which were good and just, though often unreal. Many of these films showed the good as triumphant, the bad as the defeated foe, simplistic answers were given to the difficult problems of life, a sense of reality was absent.

163

Recent years have seen film begin to deal with contemporary problems more realistically. Perhaps the Puritan ethic in film died when Steiner, the intellectual, committed suicide in *La Dolce Vita* and the cowboy lost out to society in *Lonely Are The Brave.* A sense of tragedy was experienced when the gangster-lovers, the "bad ones" were killed in *Bonnie and Clyde.*

The pathos of early films and the new movies have the same link as the new born child to its mother. From 1895 to the present, audiences have been amazed and shocked at the power of film to give a sense of reality, whether the shot of a train entering a railroad station in 1895 or the death of Ratso in *Midnight Cowboy* in 1969. The railroad and Ratso share the link of mobile images.

Though Pauline Kael calls film the "bastard art" because of the confused mixture of technicians to compose a film, there is still a human dimension to the history of film, a dimension in which the film director and film viewer attempt to make connections, a communication between two psyches. D. W. Griffith was involved in this process, so are Mike Nichols and Arthur Penn.

As in religious circles, children today are finding film content in symbols. Most parents have experienced their children shouting as the family passed a movie marquee: "Look, we can see that movie, it's a *G.*" After almost forty years of opposing film ratings, the film industry introduced a new language to the film audience: "G"—"GP"—"R"—"X". The language was developed because of local community and legislative pressure and the number of youth who were beginning to support the film industry. People felt the artistic tact of film, touching on contemporary problems with revelations recalling sex and violence, too strong for children.

Jack Valenti, president of the Motion Picture Association of America (MPAA), stated, "Our primary concern is children, and that concern is the dominant reason for the voluntary film rating system." The code was introduced as a method of warding off government censorship and preserving free expression in the arts, even if these expressions were offensive to a segment of the population. The rating is a positive approach in an industry in which there is a certain amount of exploitation, particularly by the film maker who merely produces a film for sexual exploitation.

Of all films produced by film companies and independent film makers from October 1968 to October 1970, reports *Variety,* X-rated films accounted for 7% of the film volume; R-rated films, 30%; GP-rated films, 37%; G-rated films, 26%.

A problem arises in a film in which controversial activity is important to the story and the integrity of the film's content. Often good films, because of an X-rating, will be misjudged by the non-viewer. Rating systems are guidelines, not censored listings. Some "G" films lack such quality and taste they should be prohibited from children's eyes for fear of encouraging bad taste.

Film critic Judith Crist has stated, "Classification has in many instances kept mature young people out of theaters that have been jammed by adults with ten-year-old mentalities."

The rating system fits the needs of adults and probably protects the older generation more than it does the younger audiences. The rating system will change each year; the film audience will demand it through their activity at the box office. It is ridiculous, for instance, to rate the documentary film *Woodstock* "R" ("X" in some communities), a film of youth about a youth event, because of scenes of young people "skinny dipping".

Film, as television, presents the audience with an optical illusion, the illusion of movement. Film is seeing and perceiving. The film takes on reality as the film image dissolves into the viewers life, the film, all by itself, is not reality.

As life changes so does film, its content and style. Life and film undergo constant revision. New experience in culture provides new concepts for film; both are constantly in motion, cutting from experience to experience, the velocity of life and the speed of film mirroring the world.

The power of film is its communication to the audience, not in isolation, but in the context of life after leaving the theater. Film can force the viewer to connect with himself and his world. Developing of such connections may be helped by . . .

a.  reading film critics of major magazines and local newspapers for background and perceptions related to the content of film. Critics do more than review a film, they highlight elements of film, its language, technical style, script, acting, music, and composition. Such reading serves as basic training for understanding the art of film.

b.  comparing film awards. Each year the *New York Critic's Awards* (awards for talent and skill) and the *Academy Awards* (industry awards, sometimes talent is awarded) recognize key films and actors, including directing skills and cinematography. Test your skills and train your perceptions by seeing the award winning films to analyze your ability to rate films by quality.

c. beginning a film group, one which sees the same film and meets to discuss the film in terms of story content as well as composition.

d. having the family attend the same film for family discussion purposes. This means films which the parents enjoy as well as the young people. Be open to listen to one another's concerns regarding the film. Perhaps new understanding of film and each other will be born of the experience.

e. having the local theater manager speak to a group of friends. Ask him, how does the local theater select its films . . . which films are well attended, not well attended . . . what do the selection of films have to say of the artistic level of the community . . . what are the latest trends from the production centers as revealed to him in his trade magazines?

f. seeing films.

# IX

# THE LANGUAGE OF PRINT

The visual emphasis in communication of recent years has forced the language of print to be more selective in the styles of words used and the manner of presentation of such words. Even with the competition of the visual language the printed word still counts in society.

Printed words are a medium and a message. Similar to any media, the content must be sought in the meaning and not merely the face value of the printed symbols frozen into type styles on a page. Printed words on the page lose their power when they become the primary source of information at the expense of other sources. When God can only be experienced or taught through the quotations of a book, when the book is the only medium of education, then print is a frozen experience devoid of human experience.

On the other hand, when libraries are burned down on college campuses; when books are purchased only to serve as coffee table decor; when Rod McKuen is favored over Dylan Thomas or e e cummings, then people are robbed of the beauty that can be found in printed words.

People today are less typographic than in past years dating from the time Gutenberg began handing out his moveable type handbills. In recent years educational institutions have moved from the singular use of books to film, television, filmstrips, records, as well as taking classes out into the community for an educational experience rather than only book learning.

Noted communication consultant Marshall McLuhan has said, "Consistently, the twentieth century has worked to free itself from the conditions of passivity, which is to say, from the Gutenberg heritage itself." New sources of information in society have forced print media into new efforts in publishing. More books and magazines are beginning to look like movies, with sharp integration of space, visual impact and careful selection of type style. The pages resemble a passage from scene to scene rather than chapter to chapter. Publishers are learning that space has a mood and type styles have textures, each of which aid in communicating the content of the message.

Print media is not dead, it is beginning to regain life as it stretches its horizons. The electric media has created new print concepts for the writer and the publisher. The writer today becomes a participant in the creation of a book, he no longer mails the material to a publisher and then divorces himself from the production of the material. Visual experiences have also attracted the young to the world of print and led them to read more and discover new powers in writing. The young are writing free of many of the old restrictions placed on print in terms of style, content, use of words, and the formation of the book itself.

*Concrete Poetry* offers the finest example of the new relationship between print and visual experience. This poetry is a process by which words, phrases, and syllables are isolated and placed in situations which allow them to be explored anew in combination with visual and graphic forms. Concrete Poetry is an art form born of the visual and print cultures, sharing their common significance as communication media, each needing the other, the visual semantic, and the phonetic aspects in joint community. Such experiences prevent man from becoming involved in the uniform world of a single medium of expression.

Newspapers are the schoolmasters
of the common people. That endless

book, the newspaper, is our national glory.

Henry Ward Beecher

Newspapers are the most common print experience of the majority of people in society. The freedom of the press is one of the most jealously guarded rights of American society. In establishing the first American newspaper, Benjamin Franklin listed these reasons among his objectives: "That people everywhere better understand the circumstances of public affairs, both abroad and at home, which may not only direct their thoughts at all times, but at some times also assist their business and negotiations; that something be done towards the curing, or at least the charming, of that spirit of lying, which prevails among us."

It is the responsibility of the press to inform the public of the happenings of the day and also offer insight into the significant events through in-depth analysis. It does both through *soft* and *hard* news.

Soft news offers immediate attention to the reader, it is the headline, it captures the eye of the potential reader urging him to purchase the newspaper. The soft news is the big print screaming the words of disaster, accident, crime, or the latest word of the war. Soft news may be the headline one day, and found on page 50 the next day.

Hard news is the print of information, the news which comes under close scrutiny and adds significance to the reader's understanding and growth on a particular subject. Hard news doesn't attempt to please all men, but it offers the facts and insights into a story. Such news rejects parochialism for the wide view of an event. It equips the public for the future as well as offering insight into the present.

172

Television has robbed the newspaper of its soft news, for television can easily handle the headline and first two paragraphs of most stories found on the front page of the newspaper. The future of the newspaper lies in its ability to project the content of the soft news, something the news magazine and television cannot do. The future of newspapers depends greatly on the ability to present hard news objectively, treating readers as intelligent beings, assisting them in having such information as will allow them to independently arrive at conclusions.

As newspapers are challenged into a new hard news format they face two other increasing dangers. The first is the decline of newspaper ownership. More newspapers are owned by fewer people, setting up monopolies in some areas of the society. In 1910, when the population was 92 million, there were 2,600 newspapers in the United States. Today with a population of 200 million there are only 1,700 newspapers. Some of these newspapers also own local television and radio stations, thus allowing a single person, the newspaper owner, to foist his single viewpoint over a period of time on a large segment of the population and thus influence the public for good or bad.

A second problem is newspaper's involvement with political and business structures. A newspaper with vested interests in law firms, big business, or local politics, will find it difficult to present unbiased news reports on these interests. Many newspapers have such interests today, affecting them in their responsibility to offer objective news reporting to the public.

Newspaper's involvement with special interests, or its' total support of "the establishment" has led to a rash of small newspapers being produced. Often titled "free press" or "journalism review", they are an attempt to counteract the slanted reporting of mainline newspapers.

The "underground newspaper" has also become another phenomenon of the American landscape in recent years. These newspapers offer independent voices to the newspaper scene, an opportunity for many fine writers to report news freely. Underground newspapers sometimes emerge to become important news sources in the community. *The Village Voice* of New York City has become as important a communication piece as the *New York Times.*

The newspaper has a public, one which needs to be kept informed. The newspaper must continue to observe the human landscape and prevent man from being overcome by those little lies which so often prevail in society. A reader may avoid those lies, develop sense, and renew keen perception by knowing the news of the newspaper. The reading of several newspapers, comparing the content of television news with the printed news, and seeking other sources of information, will aid an enlightened public.

A perceptive public forces the newspaper to remain honest in its reporting and sharing of information. Intelligent readers encourage reporters to be competent in the gathering and writing of the news. Sensitive readers offer the challenge of restraint to newspapers who seek to sensationalize the ugly. An aware public demands variety and opinion and opposes the narrowness of news monopolies and editorial propaganda.

My question is a simple one;
who am I to write a book? I
don't know. I'm just writing

it. You're just reading it.
Let's not worry about it.

James Simon Kunen,
*The Strawberry Statement*


More than 30,000 books are published each year to satisfy the varying needs of a reading public. The variety of material include such inane works as *The Love Machine;* sensitive biographies as *Zelda;* adventure stories as *Papillion;* memoirs as *Inside The Third Reich;* and cultural studies as *The Greening of America.*


The massive publishing efforts are met by paradoxical facts, although many more books are being published, fewer people are apparently reading books. Books may be used as decoration for the library shelf, or unwanted gifts from a monthly book club mailing. An occasional best seller may come into the hands of an individual, but there is a definite form of illiteracy in society. In 1970 *The New York Times* reported that the population is possibly "functionally illiterate," perhaps by 50%. It commented that most adults have not kept up with fourth or fifth grade reading skills, thus are unable to absorb information from print. This problem may be symbolically seen in the fact that suburban homes are generally designed without bookshelves.


Such a report indicates, perhaps, the power of mass media to turn humans away from the time-consuming tasks of intelligent growth through diligent absorption of material in the print culture, particularly the book. A look at books which become best sellers in sales and money like *The Sensuous Woman* and *The Love Machine* indicates the level of print perception among the general public.

The book as the archetype of culture is giving way to new styles of packaging experience and emotion in the content. There is a trend toward a "journalistic style" of writing, a style akin to the newspaper. People are attempting to avoid scholarly confusion and dullness for understanding. Many recent writings in books of theology reveal this style. More young writers are involved in publishing today, using fewer words, but choosing those words with care for expression and meaning. And then, the process of writer and publisher working jointly to create the book, is a new trend.

The language of books still offers unique experiences for the reader living in a multi-media world. The book provides experiences which film and television lack; the power to "turn back" the pages; time to pursue and investigate an idea or thought in the confines of the material; time to understand, to enter the mind of another and struggle with the intricate processes of thought through searching the text. Books also have the packaged availability of size for the purse and the instant presence in order to mark, underline, and reread.

The stiff print of the words in books can become fluid as the reader relates what he is reading to the life about him. To release trapped words into one's life becomes an exhilarating experience, a wondrous event for the reader.


The increased tempo of life of the contemporary world and the varieties of experience available to every human in society has been matched by the infinite variety of magazines available to the population. Printing houses publish a flood of material for every person, provide information about cars, camping, airplanes, home decorations, weekly news, service club organs, poetry, sun bathing, and even pornography. There are magazines for almost everyone's taste, magazines for intellectual growth as well as consumer buying.

The United States is perhaps the largest consumer of magazines in the world. This is due to increased leisure on the one hand, and the problem of speed on the other. Leisure allows for participation in more activity, thus more information is needed about the leisure activities. The theme of swiftness is met by providing digests of articles and the capsuling of books for fast reading.

Magazines are a serious business to most publishers, and the content of most magazines reflect such an attitude. Even the family magazine read at the supermarket counter will include articles related to birth control, abortion, politics, venereal disease, and the like. Magazines have reflected the times, offering more information of a serious nature for the reading public. The liberalization of society has also enabled magazines to include articles and information which were formerly taboo. Such inclusion makes for an informed public the possibility of deepening concern for public and private issues.

Magazines, as opposed to television and newspapers, will usually remain longer in the home, being read and reread, serving as the "instant replay" of the print media, being clipped for recipes, serving as a source for children's school reports, and as a welcome break from the television commercial.

The mass circulation magazine appeals to the broad mass of people offering pictorial views (*LIFE*) of society, news commentary (*TIME*), collections and summaries of other material (*READERS DIGEST*), male orientation (*PLAYBOY*), female concerns (*COSMOPOLITAN*), and television information (*TV GUIDE*). These magazines offer content which is very general in nature, providing quality material, yet not demanding a forceful literate skill. These magazines offer the public a variety of tastes and concerns, avoiding the selective reader or audience. The "hard hat", college professor, housewife, janitor, politician, athlete, and young person may read a mass circulation magazine with equal delight and entertainment, gaining some knowledge and insight into the world's varied environments.

The small magazine has celebrated a phenomenal rise in recent years and appeals to the select audience, often those more literate in society. Small magazines often serve as the launching pad for future writers and poets. As the mass circulation magazine depends upon advertising for funds, the small magazine will often be subsidized, by either a foundation grant or the gift from a wealthy donor or college.

Magazines will continue to entertain and enlighten the homes of America, reflecting social trends from week-to-week, providing escape and interest, and—serving as a footrest on the coffee table. This is the mixed world of the American magazine.

The following concerns are geared toward taking a look at one's relationship toward the print culture:

a. How would one analyze his favorite newspaper? What is its stance politically, economically, socially? Does it offer a balanced view of the world or merely serve as a support toward one's own personal views?

b. A 1969 Harris Poll revealed that the closer the readers are to the news the more they believe it. The report found that local news is trusted very much by 40% of the readers, state news by 31% and world news by only 25%. Do you react the same way in the reading of news—local and international?

c. Investigate the magazines of your coffee table. What do the variety of magazines indicate of your own reading habits and perception of the world? Which magazines appeal to the various levels of the family?

d. Make a list of the ten significant books you have read in your lifetime. For what reason did you select these books (content, change created in thought, entertainment)? Which book from the list would you recommend to another person, why?

e. Form a book club with neighbors and friends, selecting a book a month to read and discuss.

**X**

# THE LANGUAGE
# OF ART

The language of art is the creation of the individual, the artist. Even the corporate arts of dance, drama, and architecture are usually the result of some individual's vision and dream. The artist, through the skills of his language, offers his feelings to the world and transmits understanding by his chosen medium.

Artists do not live in vacuums, but are dependent on the psychological motifs of their times, the history of their age. Artists develop a critical stance in their society, they are a people who from birth have not been dulled by violence, automation, and professional sports; their senses have not been conquered by the disease of practicality. As artists live in the world they see a transcendent uniqueness in natural creation and in the dignity of humanity. Artists have visions of mankind, a spiritual dream born of hope, people alienated from the general thrust of the scientific emphasis of this age.

The artist does not live in the same world as the philosopher, politician, salesman, business executive, or scientist. He lives in the same environment, or culture of society, speaks the same words, yet has a world of his own. Perhaps the artist is the ordinary man intensified, and this fact alone makes him different.

As this artist then attempts to offer his feelings to the world and transmit his understandings, he doesn't necessarily communicate to all people. The artist doesn't expect all people to receive his feelings. If all people at all times and in all places understood the artist then art would be at the level of Mother Goose tales or Sallman's "Head of Christ." There would be absent from the world the magnificence of a Picasso, e e cummings, Orson Wells, or Johann Sebastian Bach.

The artist uses the materials of his trade and ventures

into the unknown. His tools may be brush, metal, pen, welding equipment, clay, camera. In each case he speaks, not quite sure where the materials will go, or what shape they have, or the content they will carry.

Because the artist confronts his feeling and creates out of the unknown, his art is often disturbing to his society. The signals he sends out are not always received. He becomes an irritant to his own people, a stranger in his own land.

The general history of the artist in mankind is one of non-acceptance and rebuke by his own culture. The works of many artists, whether it be painting, sculpture, or music, are generally praised after the artist has died.

Art then has always been in a state of crisis within its own culture. Many artists, even today, are generally accepted by the generation which is "coming along" rather than the older generation who are supposed to be bearers of culture. Many film artists, for example, are men and women over forty. Their largest audience is found in the young, their loudest critics the adult—their own generation.

Because art does not merely reproduce reality the artist becomes a divine irritant, always intimating something more in his work, forcing the viewer to make a connection, but designing the path toward the connection.

Andrew Wyeth, contemporary artist, does not reproduce the world as in a Polaroid photograph, but is often mistaken as doing just that, painting a barn like a barn and a tree like a tree. Wyeth doesn't paint people, barns, or trees, he paints feelings, emotions, understandings, most of which do not make connections with the masses of people.

Wyeth is not a Norman Rockwell, a folk artist, Wyeth's

works demand imagination, careful observation, a studied disciplined look at what is beyond the stroke of color. His are more than trees, they are figures weighted with memory and history, and his battered barns are images of older generations brooding about better days.

His "Christina's World" a painting of his polio stricken neighbor on a hillside crawling toward a grey house beyond is the story of each person, crippled in some manner, trapped in loneliness, pushed to the limits of his strength, but still groping for home. Behind Andrew Wyeth is more than a pretty picture, there is the artist speaking to society, offering his feelings and understandings. He doesn't paint landscapes, he paints humanity. Too often people see only the landscape.

The language of art is more than the appreciation of the beauty of line and form, color and space, or pan and cut. It also includes the element of perception of the artists feelings, a participation with him in the act of creation.

There is no formula for developing the perceptions of the artist. There is no path toward making simple connections with the artist except the difficult road of awareness toward self and the world which surrounds the self.

The artists today, as they deal with "Kinetic Art," "Pop Art," "Op Art," "Environmental Art," or the art of "mixing the media," are offering understandings of the world in their language. The onus of making a connection with the language lies in the viewer and participant, their ability to see this electric world which envelopes each person.

The language of art is a road which offers common people of everyday life assurance of their humanness, dreams, failures, fears, and hopes. John Dewey has said, "Art has been the means of keeping the sense of purposes that outrun evidence and of meanings that transcend indurated habit." He indicates that art, whether from the work-a-day individual involved in creative conversation or the professional artist creating new music, is central to the meaning of culture and important to the content of communication.

Art is involved in communication, for art is essentially a way of seeing, or at least a willingness to see. It is the difference between knowing and labeling; it is the ability to receive new ideas by exploring this world through personal involvement, community interest, and media perception.

Art can be the common person living in time and space, pursuing roles in an attempt to discover self in the midst of many languages and environments; it tries to make sense out of life while observing the pace of revolutions and counter revolutions; it helps develop personal philosophies and skills. As one's life becomes an "art form" experience, one connects with culture and people.

A single individual, as he attempts to communicate to a friend is a participant with the professional artist who is involved in the same process, except he does so with canvas or clay.

A knowledge of communication, its processes and conflicts, involves a sensitivity to the art of daily living. The *applied art* of the individual and the *fine art* of the artist share the same functions: the liberation of self and society to communicate, making personal connections, and the freedom of all to develop perceptions for knowing and seeing the world each day in a new light.

Anything which destroys the individuals right to know

and grow hampers the individual's opportunity toward communication, whether it be the conformity of communism or middle class materialism. Freedom to communicate is never a *right* but always a *quest,* in every society, for the artist and for the common man. Communication then, is always in crisis, for it is the constant struggle to make connections with fellow man, against the odds inflicted by every society.

# Resources

This resource listing moves beyond the mere naming of a few books. It encourages the reader to develop a library for personal study to enhance one's own growth experience as they move through this world. Communication is built on knowing and sharing. Hopefully this list offers possibilities for both.

Though the list deals with books, it encourages one to use the vast resources of film in the local theater, quality selection of television programming, the reading of magazines, listening to contemporary music, and participating in lively discussion with friends.

## PART I

*Understanding Media: The Extensions of Man,* Marshall McLuhan. McGraw-Hill. Paperback.

> This book offers perspectives of culture and environment which have shaken historians and communication experts. A primary source for understanding this world by controversial prophet and cultural philosopher, Marshall McLuhan.

*Explorations In Communications,* edited by Edmund Carpenter and Marshall McLuhan. Beacon Press. Paperback.

> An anthology of articles exploring facets of communication, including poetry, media, linguistic thought and education.

*The Greening of America,* Charles A. Reich. Random House. Hardcover.

> A view of contemporary America, its culture environments, complexities, and value systems. A mirror of present day society.

*Communications And Social Order,* Hugh Dalziel Duncan. Oxford Press. Paperback.

> A sociological study of social interaction, including theories of communication which create some of the present day problems.

*The Image,* Kenneth Boulding. Ann Arbor Paperback, University of Michigan Press. Paperback.

> Man moves primarily with images of himself and the world. This book deals with the images of man and the images of modern society.

*Culture and Commitment,* Margaret Mead. Doubleday. Paperback.

> A study of two different generations at work in society.

*The Use and Misuse of Language,* S. I. Hayakawa. Fawcett Book. Paperback.

> An excellent study containing material on speaking, hearing, the language of pictures, and other concerns of contemporary communication.

# PART II

*Watch Your Language*, Theodore M. Berstein. Pocket Books. Paperback.

> A delightful book offering instructive information regarding the use of words in writing and speaking.

*Prime Time, The Life of Edward R. Murrow*, Alexander Kendrick. Avon Press. Paperback.

> Through the life of this great man one sees the potential power of radio and television.

*How To Talk Back To Your Television Set*, Gay Talese. Bantam Books. Paperback.

> The inside story of the workings of the New York Times demonstrates the mechanisms of the modern day newspaper.

*The Selling of the President*, Joe McGinniss. Pocket Books. Paperback.

> Report of the use of media in packaging a presidential candidate. Demonstrates the power of media to sell people.

*Expanded Cinema*, Gene Youngblood. A Dutton Paperback.

> Excellent book dealing with the electronic age and

media, its potentials in the future as well as philosophies regarding their use.

*The Liveliest Art,* Arthur Knight. A Mentor Book. Paperback.

A primary book of film history, demonstrating the role this language has played in the world.

*Pop Culture in America,* edited by David Manning White. A Quadrangle Paperback.

An attempt to understand the popular tastes of American culture. A fine survey of popular culture as opposed to fine art.

*Art and Alienation,* Herbert Read. Viking Compass Book. Paperback.

Content deals with its title, offering glimpses into various artists, their works, and role in society.

*Toys Toys Toys,* R. Paul Firnhaber and Paul A. Schreivogel. Augsburg Publishing House. Hardcover.

A sociological look at toys as environmental media and communication tools.